W9-BEV-035

I'M NOT MOVING OUT

I'M NOT GETTING A JOB

SCREW YOU:

A Millennial Field Guide

+ Gen Z

Written by Dario CiVon

Dario CiVon

Copyright © 2018 Dario CiVon

All rights reserved.

ISBN: 9781729131602

DEDICATION

Dedicated to my amazing Mom and Dad who have given me the freedom to grow, explore, and become my own person without (too much) meddling.. Thank you dearly.

TABLE OF CONTENTS

ACKNOWLEDGEMENTS

I must acknowledge: The inventors of the Internet. Whoever you are. Secondary to them: YouTube, Google, Tumblr, Instagram, Business Insider, and TEDx.

Thank you to Art Center College for having some amazing faculty members that have encouraged me on this project.

My creative inspirations: Bobby McFerrin, Jim Carrey, Mark Manson, and George Carlin who have given me the creative courage to write this book.

I also must thank my best friends, Sam Baldwin, Christopher SooHoo, Jack Hale, and Jocelyn Sepulveda for sharing many amazing conversations with me over the years. We talk about some of the most esoteric and hard to answer questions of life. We also talk about stupid stuff too, both of which are important to be able to do with the people around you. I have expanded my mind tremendously through their ability to communicate how their brains works.

I have to give a special thank you to Tai Lopez for changing my life. His online programs which he aggressively markets towards Millennials have given me the frameworks and daily routines to actually get shit done. I would not have had the perseverance to write this book without joining his 67 Steps program, which is the most practical collection of wisdom available about life in the modern world. I also have to thank Gary Vaynerchuk, Investor and CEO of Vaynermedia, who has informed me and empowered me (through his Instagram and daily video diary). His videos never fail to light a fire under my ass when I'm dragging my feet. Duncan Trussel, for his fascination in converting Eastern wisdom into modern terminology. The late Terrence McKenna, one of the most fascinatingly eloquent speakers ever for his deep insights into the nature and purpose of life. Joe Rogan (stand-up comedian/podcaster) who is a true hero of mine. If you're over 40, you know him as the 'Fear Factor guy'. But Millennials know him as one of the top podcasters in the world. His combination of intelligence, curiosity, wit, analyses, individualism, and childishness is a something I strive for in life.

And most important of all, I have to thank my wonderful parents who have supported me in all of my endeavors. They are encouraging, critical, and have always given me ample space to become my own person. Thank you… for everything.

Chapter 1:
MY EXTENSIVE QUALIFICATIONS

My name is Dario CiVon, a 24 year-old millennial blend of a human being. My father grew up in the Midwestern rust belt and my mother is the daughter of a Central American politician and an international concert pianist. A mix of English, Irish, German, Ukranian, and Spanish. So, I'm just a regular ol'American Millennial. A middle class, suburban kid, whose parents are TV writers.

I still live with them, and I haven't had a 'real' job yet. I've always been a strange mix of extrovert and introvert; an intellectual with a taste for the absurd. I went to a well ranked public high school in California and got mostly A's, (and mostly C's in math.) I'm athletic, but nothing overly special. Well, I was the starting shooting guard on my high school basketball team, which was *just* shy of winning the state championship in 2011... So clearly, I got some friggin' knowledge about life... ☺

But what qualifies me to write a book, you ask? How about my sterling educational background? Well... like so many Millennials, I chose the wrong college out of high school, because I had no freaking idea what really mattered to me, and because school was so uninspiring and procedural. ☹ I quickly recognized my choice for what it was: sixty grand a year of partying and drinking.

To supplement this lackluster education my parents were mostly paying for, I spent about 300 hours studying... uhh... 'liberal arts' with the Joe Rogan Experience Podcast on the side. Here, I was introduced to experts, comedians, authors, scientists and high achievers in almost every field. I got to hear them speak in depth about how *they* found meaning in their life for three hours at a time. And it was free! A vast curiosity for the world and for philosophy was instilled in me through hearing these people. And I started to feel inspired to follow in the great tradition of public discourse.

I would go on YouTube 'journeys' for hours and hours trying to wrap my head around the sheer diversity of the human experience that was boggling my nineteen-year-old mind. Along the way I studied a modern take on Buddhism and simulation theory with the Duncan Trussel Family Hour Podcast, and became an avid fan of the lectures of the late philosopher Terrence McKenna.

All of this thinking eventually lead me transfer to one of the top design schools in the country, Art Center College. But if I was ever going to make impactful art at a large scale, I needed to learn about business. So I began studying business on the side with the Tai Lopez Online Business Accelerator Program. Basically, a gigantic library of lectures and book summaries. I quickly learned just how poor my life skills really were. Tai Lopez, famous for having read a book per day for over a decade, showed me how to divide my time, how to organize my life, how to plan my goals, how to figure out what my goals should even be, the importance of constant learning, and much more. It was a life-changing crash-course in life skills, none of which were taught to me in school.

After two years of sleepless nights listening to shit online while studying draftsmanship and painting with a focus on Entertainment Design at Art Center, I took a leave of absence to work on my first book...ahem... this one.

You were worried about my credentials weren't you? Well, this is what an intellectually curious, younger-ish Millennials education looks like. A glorious hodge-podge form high quality online resources.

4 REALZ THO... I've been an avid internet researcher my entire life. I've studied a good bit of science, technology, and biology, art, sociology, history, philosophy, and of course Art! (The one that tries to give meaning to them all alright?) I love thinking about the macro picture. The only point of view which I am loyal to.

And so with that said, I have a huge desire to talk about young people from a broader perspective; to explain the bigger picture. **To consolidate all the dialogue and anxieties about millennials in one place.**

I think most 'real adults' are behind the times. They aren't fully comprehending just what the internet is, and how it's affecting *our* world view. They don't get it! And so it is my Millennial duty to share *our* perspective through this field guide. And for any Millennials reading, I'm also going to toss out some advice/moments of clarity that I've had along my journey through multiple institutions, desperately trying to cope with complexity of modern life. Hopefully you'll find some of these tips insightful.

Admittedly, I'm not an expert in -- well, anything really. But what I do feel qualified to talk about is *how* having access to the internet has changed my psyche and how it is effecting the psyche of my entire generation. In a visceral way... **How the internet, video games, social media, are shaping our minds, and our world!**

Don't worry, I speak 'adult' fluently, though I can't guarantee there won't be errors in the translation. Or the occasional techno-quasi-Buddhistic-theosophical outburst... I apologize in advance.

I hope to convey how these technologies are fostering the development of a new kind of person. One who is more globally minded, more empathetic, and more visual than any generation before. How having access to information 24/7 is acting like fertilizer to the young intellect, if used responsibly. And how the internet is cultivating a certain healthy open mindedness. I want to defy the stereotype that the internet is *only* used for posting selfies and watching cat videos.

Sure, there's plenty of that, but there's also a ton of learning and meta-analysis that goes on subconsciously, which Millennials then bring to all aspects of their life.

I'm also going to take a brief stab at explaining how I think Millennials will reshape religion, politics and finance. But I'll keep it short and non-political. (Ugh...politics).

So hopefully, by the end of this book you'll at least have some sense of *why* we Millennials act the way we do, speak using meme-lingo, feel the things we do, and amuse ourselves with the most absurd content you can imagine. Why we are motivated differently than prior generations. What the psychological lenses by which we view the world are... and what it truly means to have the internet as the central vehicle for our entire life.

By no means will I be able to account for the beliefs of everyone. Millennials, like any generation of people, are diverse. And those of us who are pretty much digital natives like myself, are probably a little different than the older ones.

These are my opinions based on my experiences with my peers growing up amidst the blossoming information age. I will try to paint with a reasonably broad brush (cuz im an artist) but I'm sure that not every Millennial will agree with me on *everything*. I'm also going to try and 'check my privilege', but it may pop in from time to time.

Think of me like a helpful Millennial Sherpa trying to **bridge the culture gap** between Millennials and the people who roamed the earth before ubiquitous internet, in your pants. Namaste :)

Do not fear, I don't suffer from Millennial over sensitivity syndrome (did you read the title?) I'm not in a sanctioned 'safe room', though I have written most of this from my parent's kitchen table. I'm not afraid to be critical of our generation, and I will definitely point out some of the weaknesses I see in myself and others.

Will this book be snarky? Yes. Will you learn why I think it's good that many of us are living at home? Yes. And will I give some advice on how to handle college these days? Yes. Will this book piss you off if you're over fifty and very traditionally oriented? Probably. Am I sorry? Kinda/not. But I'll try to back up my reasoning with some sense of logic, and understanding for different viewpoints.

Seriously, when I do sound like a snarky Millennial it's really only to drive home one key point: that *everything* about the way we *do* everything is changing. **We are in the middle of one the most transformative periods in human history.** The internet is quite literally reshaping the way everything on planet Earth operates. As we speak.

This reshaping is facilitating an open minded and efficient, globally cohesive society the likes of which we haven't seen before on this rock'. And for the sake of the polar bears, we need to do it fast!

OH YA... MY TITLE... PROBLY SHOULD EXPLAIN...

"I'm not moving out, I'm not getting a job, screw you" is what many non-Millennials implicitly feel when they hear that roughly 40% of Millennials are living at home or with a family member. This is where the whole, "living in their parents' basement" stereotype comes from that we hear all the time. "Millennials are losers, they're lazy, they're spoiled"... Yadda yadda yadda...

Millennial's want good wages and self sufficiency as much as anyone. As a Millennial that has lived with his parents through college, I can attest, it is no one's first choice.

Over the course of this book, I'm going to explain why living with your folks has its downsides, but also why more people should actually embrace it. I want to de-stigmatize the process of figuring out your life in these changing times, and respectfully, say 'buzz off' to anyone who doesn't understand the factors at play.

Rapidly escalating rents, stagnant wages, and crippling student debt have made living with you're parents the best option if you can do it. And in fact, it should be encouraged. Why?

Because, underneath the quarterly peaks and valleys of our economic charts, a deeper trend is brewing. **As I've said, the world is changing**. It is restructuring around a superior organizational system, i.e. the internet and software renaissance. And it's having it's effect on the job market faster than colleges can possibly adjust.

Already, my chosen profession, Concept Design for games, has been technologized far beyond what I could have imagined when I started four years ago. **I've literally had to adjust my formal education three times to stay up-to-date.**

Which means I'm having to learn new software constantly, while I'm also learning design fundamentals. **Because the way that academic knowledge is being applied is changing so freakin' fast.**

This is both good, and bad. The good is that technical skills and high strategic/team intelligence have been prioritized. Both of which you don't necessarily need a degree to acquire anymore. But this is bad if you are paying a hefty price for a degree that may enlighten you, but will leave you without specialized skills needed for a decent-paying job.

As I see it, we are living on the tail end of a college degree bubble. With the rise of badass, **constantly updating, online learning platforms** -- and YouTube -- the value of what many colleges offer is decaying while the prices keep rising. Which is why college enrollment has been declining for the last five years. Many of the 'hard skills' of college can now be learned online now, probably more efficiently. (Not recommending this if you want to be a surgeon).

For general education, business, and programming, there are sites like MIT's OpenCourseWare, Stanford Online, Edx, and Khan Academy. And the courses are amazing! It's also possible to find curriculums for most colleges courses online.

Also, there are industry specific platforms that have sprung up in nearly every niche specializing in teaching specific tools that employers need.

All of these methods are severely threatening the in-person college experience because they are relatively cheap, and really good. And many people are becoming unwilling to strap themselves with so much crushing debt. In my field of art, there are sites like The Gnomon Workshop, DigitalTutors, NewMastersAcademy, or LearnSquared-- all taught by dozens of working professionals using the most current tools of the trade.

These were the conversations I found myself having with my fellow students as we sat in unnecessary curriculum-padding classes, paying an arm and a leg, begging for it to be over so we could focus on the stuff that really mattered to us. And keep in mind I *mostly* liked my (second) college.

Then there's MissionU, which I think is the higher educational model of the future (no, they are not paying me for this plug). It's a one-year intensive set of courses in data analytics (one of the most sought after and future-proof professions in America). Here's the thing: it's **entirely free** until you land a job that pays you $50,000 or more per year. At which point, you pay 15% of your income to them for the next three years. So if they fail you, they don't get paid a dime. That kind of accountability doesn't exist in the traditional college system. They already have a dozen large corporate partners who have pledged to hire MissionU grads.

Or you can go Elon Musk-style: just buy college textbooks and read them. That's what my programmer friend, Steve did before starting his own start-up.

But this means that Millennials are living/lived in the 'awkward period' as I call it. Many of us have paid for a degree in something, but haven't been taught the specific skills to make us desirable in the **actual real world**. Or, there is just so much parity between individuals with shiny diplomas it's hard to even get someone to read your resume. Ironically, it's these online courses taught by specialists that actually give you the edge. Not the degree...

So, we are left to 'skill up' on our own... after college.

And that's why any extra time that a Millennial can have to study the trends and future-proof their skills, is time well spent. If that means locking yourself in your room for six months and becoming an expert in a specific piece of new software, go do it! And if that means living with our parents for a while... then Mom, I want spaghetti tonight!

So, now you see where my catchy, salacious, click-bait-ey title is coming from.

This is the college experience of the future. Buffet style. I have pretty much custom-built my education utilizing both real professors and online resources to learn from the best people I could. Where my college was strong, I ruthlessly cherry picked the best classes with a Napoleonic determination. Where my college was weak, (in some cases non-existent) I supplemented using online resources. Forgoing a degree, but saving a *ton* of money. This type of combo-education has made my vision for myself broader and more eclectic, and so far, at least, I'm very happy that I forged this path. This wouldn't have been advisable even three years ago. But now, it is.

But I'm not alone. My friend Steve, a computer programmer left college halfway through in favor of reading textbooks and studying online on his own (from better teachers then his college provided.) My friend Jane got hired half way through college, after she had learned enough to land a full-time job. My brother's close friend got a law degree -*hated every second of it*-took an eight week course in programming and is now traveling the world working as a freelance coder; working from his laptop, surfing the best waves in the world, between Skyping with his clients.

My advice: go to a campus for a year or two, make relationships with the best professors -- **learn how to learn** -- and then go out and keep learning for the rest of your life from the copious resources the world has to offer. And don't come out bloated with debt!

*Disclaimer****: I can hear the voices of all the parents, Baby Boomers and Gen X'ers screaming at me through this book. To prove your concerns are heard, I've created the 'Concerned Elder', who will be calling me out on a regular basis.*

Concerned Elder: How can you say these things?! In my day a college education was the ticket to a better life?

I get it. But in your day, the cost of living was much lower in big cities. An organic vegan bison burger wasn't $12. Jobs were plentiful, employers offered benefits from the get go. An increasing number of full time gigs have become 'contract' work, and at many companies, unpaid internships are the new norm.

In a recent survey by Citizens Bank, 57% of Millennials report that they regret how much they borrowed for college. Worse yet, over a third say they wouldn't even have gone to college if they had realized in advance the true price tag of their education. Also, student debt is the only type of debt that is untouchable by bankruptcy.

The good news is: you no longer need to go to a "traditional college" to get a great education, to be skilled, super smart, and hirable. If you're still not convinced, I will expand on this topic later in the book.

P.S. Thank you for purchasing this book. All proceeds go to 'Dario's moving out fund'. I don't have a tip jar but I do except Bitcoins, Ripple, and TRON.

Chapter 2:
MILLENNIAL STEREOTYPES

WE ARE A VERY MALIGNED GENERATION. Here is a list of some of the Millennial stereotypes we constantly hear:

- we aren't tough enough/we're snowflakes (Meh)
- we are oversensitive because we *all* got trophies as kids (Not exactly true)
- we expect everyone around us to be supportive of our feelings and accepting of everything we do (Doesn't everyone want that?)
- our parents have convinced us we are more special/gifted than we actually are (Perhaps...)
- we *all* live at home with our parents (35%-45% depending on where you look)
- we are very close to our families (Yep. Over 50% of Millennials consider their mom or dad one of their best friends)
- And 54% of Millennial parents say one of their kids is their best friend (Factz)
- we tend to be very stressed out (Very true.)
- we aren't so good in face to face conversations, (But in text we're charming and witty)
- we spend waaaaaaay to much time on our devices (Can't deny that one)
- we don't prioritize job titles (Yep)
- we don't do well with strict hierarchies, or bosses (That's what happens when your parents are your best friends!)
- we like to reinvent the way things have been done before us (Yes, becuz INTERNET)
- we like having fun too much, we aren't serious enough (Cool)
- we tend to be socialistic, and want to help others (FEEL THE BERN!)
-we want our job to help the world, or else we **DGAF**. (That means: *don't give a fuck..)*
- we are idealists and not realists. We all want the world to be perfect (Guilty)
- we value experiences over money (Been to Peru?)
- we are very open to other cultures and ways of life (Because of the melting pot of the

internet)???
- we care about the health of the Earth (What a terrible thing!)
- we are very accepting of all forms of sexualities, gender and race... (Cuz more of us are gender fluid, neutral, bi, and mixed race than ever before ourselves!)
- we are less formally religious (Yes)
- we are familiar with a broad range of subject matter, albeit superficially (Because of the internet)
- we are snarky and sarcastic (Cuz of those darn internet memes)
- **we love the internet like a family member (AMEN)**

Of course *all* these traits are not true of *all* Millennials. But actually, in my experience many of these stereotypes have some truth to them. To me, someone who is kind, open to new ideas, sensitive to other's feelings, and wants to help the world sounds like a great person to be around!

Concerned Elder: You're a bunch of snowflakes who can't handle adversity!

No! Let me explain! It is more nuanced than that.

It starts with the **five key factors** that have synergized to fundamentally shape the Millennial psyche. Take note that these factors did not exist prior to our generation, in any form resembling what they are now.

1: Overly Supportive and Protective Parenting (helicopter parents)
2: The Internet
3: Social Media
4: Videogames
5: Abundance and radical improvements to Marijuana (applies to many but not all Millennials)

These are powerful stimuli! **Millennials have grown up in conditions that have never before existed in the history of the world.**
Concerned Elder: Sounds like a scary cocktail...

All five of these areas have taken exponential leaps during our youth, including marijuana. Trust me, you guys, weren't smoking the same stuff we are. (More on this later..)
Hopefully, I can deconstruct the effects of these in a way you can understand.

24/7 access to information and instant communication has led to a more sporadic mind, admittedly, but also a mind that's more open to adjustments and group thinking. We're known for being very open to change. We want to support each other, because we are constantly aware of each other through our phones which we adore, and which keep getting better and better. We want technology to solve our problems. We want to fix the world, and by and large we believe we can. (And some of us mean well, but are nervous wrecks, and have no idea where to start. More on them later)

I'm going to break down our collective psyche and along the way discuss why living with our parents for longer isn't a sign of weakness, but actually a great opportunity for people to be able to create meaningful work earlier in their life. (Like this book. Thanks mom ☺ I still want Spaghetti.)

I want you to understand where we are coming from. Why we are so interested in creating positive impact with our jobs. Why we all talk like we are mini therapists. What the hell a 'meme' is, and how they have affected our sense of humor drastically.

To that end, if my writing style feels a tad scattered and 'fitful', then good. Because that's part of the message. We love jumping around, we love connecting seemingly disparate ideas, because that's what we've grown up doing our entire lives on the internet.

Chapter 3:
THE EFFECT OF OVERLY SUPPORTIVE PARENTING

LOOK AT WHAT YOU'VE DONE

So, why are Millennials thought of *as* over sensitive? Why are we called snowflakes? What's up with the puppy parties? Micro-aggressions? Triggers? The Anxiety Epidemic. Well, a lot of this over-sensitivity has to do with a distinctive shift in parenting style.

Concerned Elder: Oh, so you're blaming your parents? What else is new?

What's new is the rise of OVERLY protective and OVERLY supportive parenting in the 1980's.

Concerned Elder: Well *ex-cuuuse* us!

I was born in 1992. Here are some things that my friends and I never heard growing up:
- "Go out and play. Come home when it's dark."
- "Children are meant to be seen and not heard."
- "You'll do it because I said so!"
- "Get me something to hit you with."
- "I'm not your friend, I'm your parent."
- "Shut up kid!"
- "I don't care what you think!"

Our parents were the first generation of Americans to openly admit that they loved their kids. As opposed to the old style of "Of course I love you. Why do I have to say it?"

I'm not saying that all Baby Boomer's parents weren't affectionate. But Baby Boomers have taken it to a whole new level. They have been much more involved with their children every step of the way, and have consciously let their child into their own psyche a lot more. Therefore their kids, Millennials, have felt comfortable to do the same. We actually talk to each other like human beings.

My dad says that he didn't hear his father say he loved him until he was thirty-three years old. He had to lock his father in the car, and wouldn't let him out until he said it! He says that his parents lived in the era of the 'unflinching exterior'. According to him, most working class men wanted to portray themselves as tough and unaffected by emotions. This style gave way as Baby Boomers had kids. Maybe it was the effect of the hippies. Maybe it was a conscious choice. Either way, many-a-Millennial has been a therapist for their parents at least a few times in their life. In fact, according to a massive poll by Fusion, 51% of Millennials now say that one of their parents is their best friend. That's nuts! I wouldn't call my parents my best friends, but they are good pals of mine ;p

Concerned Elder: Hey, it is nice to talk to someone you trust.

Millennials' parents were also much, much more protective than the prior generations. Some have traced this to an increase in crime reporting on television starting from the 1960's to the 2000's. Televised stories of murders and abducted children may have caused adults to pull in the reins.

As mothers entered the work force more, parents began enrolling their children in after school day care programs, or hiring babysitters to watch over their kids, even into their teenage years. This, plus the power of computer and videogames to keep kids inside, and so called 'free range children' have become a rarity, especially in middle class neighborhoods.

Others have pointed to the rise of the 'play date' as a large contributing factor to the 'helicopter parenting' phenomenon. As soon as parents started booking appointments for their children to play, they inevitably started increasing their involvement. They 'hovered' to control the interactions, as opposed to the old ways of letting their kids roam freely throughout the neighborhood, climb trees, get in fights, work out their differences, run from stray dogs, -- yikes -- talk to strangers!

Couple this with the 'self-esteem movement', a philosophy that spread through parenting circles in the early 80's. It advocated that parents should promote their children's pride in themselves, first and foremost. This would give them 'the confidence *they need* to achieve their goals!' This of course, led to the much maligned 'participation awards' that everyone likes to point to for ruining our competitive spirit. Or school assignments where we had to 'write down the three best attributes of all your classmates'. And there you have it!

But there's another culprit! It's the trophies, and dopamine rewards of videogames that are truly to blame for rewarding people for accomplishing absolutely nothing except have a good time. Now, don't get me wrong, I *looove* me some games. I have a whole chapter defending them, and I want to work in the industry for gosh sakes! But no doubt they *can* get in the way of progressing in the real world, as any Millenial or Gen X'er will tell you.

Millennial's also grew up with an increasing awareness of emotional trauma, stress, divorce, financial issues and anxiety. The Columbine shootings, and other horrific events, put mental health at the forefront of our parent's and our school's minds. Schools started to become more 'aware' of their students emotional state. This meant more guidance counselors, school therapists, nurses, and teachers who were instructed to be more compassionate.

As Millennials got older, the extreme emphasis that college places on grades and extra-curricular activities, kept many kids either at home doing homework, or at functions after school. Which means that for the majority of our lives we have been surrounded by adults who are emotionally sympathetic towards us. Which I think is great. But the end result is -some Millennials that have been emotionally over-protected and over insulated. **Many of us haven't had enough experience directing our own lives.** It's just been one thing to the next to the next.

A contributing factor to this over-scheduling is that many Baby Boomers, (who are also known as the 'Me' generation), viewed their children as a reflection of their own achievements.

So, starting in kindergarten, many of our parents sought to have the brightest, most 'gifted', 'college-equipped', 'future-ready' kid. They saw to it by assiduously booking music lessons, riding lessons, art lessons, Kumon, private math tutoring, peewee soccer, Y-winners basketball, Little League, scouting, you name it. During the same period, the requirements to make it into a good college kept on getting higher and higher… leading to a whole bunch of stressed out kids who define themselves by grades and test scores, and not their personal sovereignty.

All of this this left many of my generation with little time to simply wander around and play - free from adults – free from the burden of the next benchmark we had to meet. Many of us spent our evenings exploring the internet more than the real world.

Concerned Elder: If my parents knew some of the stuff I got into --

That's what I'm saying! Many youngsters don't have much experience in the real world by the time they leave high school… you know… with adults who don't give a shit about them. Many of us probably spent too much time indoors. I know most of my 'personal exploration time' was online, or inside of a videogame world. When something went wrong, you got a do-over.

Everything Millennials did as kids was highly stimulating, social media, TV, videogames, movies. I love all of those things, but there is a cost. I think that some of us feel like it's not 'ok' for things to go totally wrong. Or to completely fail at something (because we associate it with a permanent stain on our GPA or resume). As author Mark Manson puts it, "We have forgotten that it's ok for things to suck sometimes".

When this happens, we will search for emotional support online in order to feel 'accepted' rather than use the pain to help us get 'tougher'. Or we coddle ourselves into thinking everything is ok all the time. And this is where the perceived lack of toughness comes from.

In short, some of y'all might have taken your job of parenting a *little* too seriously. Keeping us regimented, and 'on track' for a college career has kept some of us from learning to handle problems on our own. It doesn't help that we are constantly seeing *everyone else's* success on social media, and the results are that Millennials are the most sensitive to stress of any generation on record.

Concerned Elder: Snowflakes…

Actually, psychologists call this 'lowered frustration tolerance'. Or, the inability to cope with frustration on your own without seeking help. Couple this with **the profound effect of being able to find emotional support online for absolutely *anything*.**

It goes like this: a Millennial will have an issue, whether it's a mental health problem, real or perceived abuse, anything… and they will find a community of other people online who have gone or are going through the same thing. In one way, this is good because they feel reassured they're not alone. But now that they have a sense of belonging because their supported in that group. There's no urgency to get past whatever issue their facing. Or sometimes, the group convinces them that there's no need to get past it at all. For some people, it can lead to a wallowing in your new community. It can lead to a sense of entitlement, or an over-aggressive sense of 'ownership' when it comes to their emotions. *"Yes, I'm easily triggered, deal with it".*

Again, this isn't all of us. But it *is* some of us and it is fucking annoying sometimes. Look, online support groups are mostly great. I think the increased awareness of each other's emotions is a terrific thing. But it can obviously be taken too far.

Psychology in general, is something I've found most Millennials have read a lot about on the internet. Because, let's face... we all suffer from something. Or at least have a tendency towards a particular neurosis. I like that we're owning up to this fact as a culture now. I think all of this supportiveness is actually a good thing if it's not taken to extreme levels of Groupthink and GroupCoddle. We want a society that is supportive and aware, right?

Anyway, all of this has shaped our expectations of adults. We subconsciously *expect* them to be supportive of us. To care about our feelings. To tolerate our quirks, our triggers, our food limitations, and to at least listen when we have a concern; because we've all read up on our own problems and own them.

Concerned Elder: Is that why you're driving your bosses crazy, telling them personal stuff they'd rather not know?

Yes. Millennials really appreciate bosses or elders who let us share our emotions with them. Empathy is something we hold at a premium.

POLITICAL CORRECTNESS & COLLEGE

Based on the number of emotional meltdowns I've seen at school over the years, I can attest to this: we Millennials *definitely* don't mind sharing our feelings with each other. And social media, for better and for worse, has made it tremendously easy to vent at a moment's notice. But it *can* get out of hand.

It's now incredibly easy to quickly create 'mini' movements on social media, for or against anything. They can sweep through a campus like wildfire. Sometimes they are totally, 1000% valid, like social outrage against racist fraternity chants. Sometimes they are not valid... like when a professor is wrongfully targeted for talking about a difficult topic that inadvertently 'triggers' the most sensitive kid in class, who can then spread exaggerated claims on Facebook, putting the professor under wrongful scrutiny.

Fellow students support these movements, because it makes them feel good to fight for something or someone. Outrage feels good sometimes. Sometimes it's warranted. Other times it's what I call 'misguided over-empathy'.

As a Millennial who prides himself on being reasonable, I worry that these rapid-fire outrage festivals will eventually make it impossible to talk about truly tough issues. Some problems can't be summed up into some politically correct little jingle. **Some issues are abrasive as heck to all parties.** But we have to be able to discuss them openly if we ever hope to fully deconstruct them. And I worry that social-media-fueled-uproar - culture will stop those forums from ever happening in the first place.

Universities are increasingly at the mercy of their most sensitive students. 'Violations' spread so quickly. The last thing any school wants to be known for is insensitivity or for being exclusionary. Especially since their demographic tends to be liberal thinking, progressive youngsters. So, they take bold measures in the opposite direction, like providing kitten parties after the election, or making professors include 'anxiety trigger warnings' in their lectures.

Concerned Elder: Pu-leeeeze...

It's important to remember *most* Millennials are not hyper-sensitive. Some are. Do I personally think emergency kitten parties are a bit much? Yes. Do a lot of us think so? Yes. Because there is a whole other type of Millennial. The type that inhales odd internet content all day long. Like this:

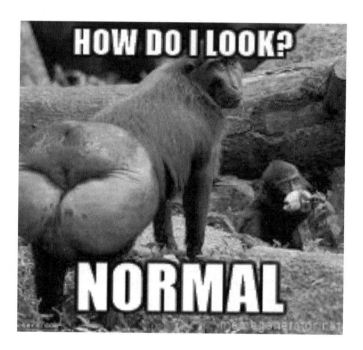

Concerned Elder: WTF?

(It gets MUCH more odd, but I'll spare you.)

Here is The Great Millennial Dichotomy:

While all Millennials are generally more empathetic to each other's emotions, **ironically, many of us are very desensitized in some ways**. We are the most sensitive and caring generation ever, and yet we have seen more weird videos, strange pictures, pornography, and other junk than any generation ever before.

So there's a spectrum of Millennials. Those of us who are very sensitive, and are easily 'triggered'. And who am I to judge them? I don't know the stuff they've been through. But then there is the snarky, jaded Millennial, who has seen so much shit online, watched enough movies, and played enough violent videogames to be anything *but* easily triggered. Full disclosure: I am one of those.

It doesn't mean we aren't in favor of equality, and/or providing emotional support for the sensitive others. I am very much so. We are just less emotional in how we go about it. We've seen enough junk online to prove that neuroses and regressive behavior are rife in this world (unfortunately). It doesn't mean we accept it, it just means when we encounter it in real life we aren't shocked by it. Most Millennials fall somewhere in the middle of this spectrum.

The overall movement towards empathy is a good thing. Our level of caring has profound implications for the future despite the occasional instances of outraged college students causing a stir. As long as it doesn't go too far, this modern ethos is gradually leading to a culture of 'let's support each other' and 'everyone deserves a fair shot'.

And the shift has a lot to do with the way we were raised. So, congratulations Concerned Elders and stop complaining about it! LOL

Here is a recurring theme of this book: I can't defend everything that Millennials do and feel, but I firmly defend the process in which this generation is partaking in. The process of being more connected and more supportive of each other. As I will explain further, I think Millennials and Gen Z are a different breed of human. With new expectations and a new, interconnected worldview. We're like Hippies 2.0, armed with apps, instant access to information, live streaming, and an entrepreneurial spirit.

The internet, social media, and videogames are truly some of the most amazing things ever to be achieved on this planet (other than warm cookies), and Millennials grew up right alongside them. It's almost like we were the test subjects in a really crazy experiment. Here are the results....

Chapter 4:
THE MILLENNIAL MIND: The Internet Effect

It seems like many older folks---er, Concerned Elders, view the internet as a tumorous lesion growing upon the rotting testicle called planet Earth. Their minds are polluted with radio hosts exclaiming how our privacy is being violated, how our information is being sold, how the internet is decaying everyone's mind, and yes, how it's being used by certain factions to further their own terrible agendas. Of course, these issues exist and they suck. But to young people, the internet is so much more than that. There is *genuine love* between us.

The internet represents total freedom! I asked my friends to describe the internet in one word.

Jane: "Endless..."
Steve: "Infinite"
Will: "Symbiosis"
Christoph: "Faucet of exposure"
(Ok, Christoph cheated, but his answer was too good to condense)

Ask any Millennial, and they would say the internet is as essential to their life as water. For me, the internet has been *as* big a part in shaping who I am as any other factor. It's been like a third parent who has shown me more about the world than any parent ever could *or would*. It's made me far more curious and knowledgeable because so much darn stuff has passed through my eyeballs!

The internet has shown me the wonderful spirit of tribal unity and dance, (something we are sorely lacking in the West). It's shown me the horrible conditions by which some of our products are manufactured. I've been blessed with access to every single piece of classical art on the planet. It's made available troves of knowledge about any era, and topic. AND, more importantly, it's a way for curators of such material to teach others about it. (Which is probably the most profound thing.)

It's also made me more empathetic for one simple reason: every single day, I get to actually see and hear TONS of other people laughing, talking and living other lifestyles than my own.

They say a picture is worth a thousand words... Well your average twenty-something has probably already consumed several libraries full of images and videos.

As far as education goes, there is tons of information out there on thousands of subjects taught by fantastically certified people. There is almost no excuse for being completely ignorant about *anything* anymore. There are hundreds of amazing sites on any topic. Lectures from the top minds in every field; from entrepreneurship, to physics, to psychology, to business--you name it. That's exciting if you don't let it overwhelm you (which is easily possible).

I think some people my age take this access for granted. But I am just old enough to remember how slow and shitty the internet was when it first came out. So, I can understand how awesome it has become. (Remember those noisy dial-up modems?)

I love the internet so much I wrote write a poem about it.

I've seen the Amazon overflowing in the spriiiiiiiiiiiiiiing,
I've heard pods of blue whales siiiiiiiiiiiiing,

I've learned so much about outer spaaaaace!
From Neil Degrasse Tyson's beautiful faaaace

I didn't know World War 1 was quite so suuucky,
Man, oh man, I just feel so luuucky,

To watch porn stars do stuff I can't repeat,
Then listen to Harvard lecture's while I eaaaaat!

I broke my habit of pro-crasti-nation,
After I watching a TED talk on proper relaxation,

I've learned Genghis Kan was a real piece of shiiiit,
Who made Hitler seem like an average misfiiiit

These are all the things that I now know!
From searching Youtube high and low!...

Ok, you get the point.

I think Millennial's literally look at the internet like a giant brain from which we can all download information. Or maybe like a giant nipple that we can all suckle knowledge out of all at once, like infants.

We are all children of the Earth after all, right? Children who need to grow strong on knowledge, philosophy, science, and perspective. And the internet is the best source for all four of those lovely things, with little regard for nationality, ethnicity, or social class. We all have this mental image of a pool of endless knowledge that everyone can drink freely from. And we know that other Millennials are on it all day long, too! It's something that unites us! Which is amazing, and a completely new layer to the human experience.

Concerned Elder: I get it. You like the internet!

Well, I think this is partially why Millennials are opposed to strict corporate hierarchies. Especially, when we can tell our boss has no idea about an entire body of knowledge located somewhere online.

Concerned Elder: What about wisdom and experience? Doesn't that count for something?

Of course there is value and authority in genuine experience. But if you don't *really know* the answer firmly, then let me go online and see how others have solved the problem. Let me see what the best people in the world think. Instead of guessing about things, let's just look it up as a team!

While watching a documentary on the Middle Ages, I was shocked to learn that there were guilds of craftsman that took blood oaths of secrecy to protect their techniques. Even the formulas for mortar and cement were highly guarded at times. You know, so those jerks across the English channel wouldn't have a better cathedral. You had masons rubbing shoulders with carpenters, who intermingled with blacksmiths, and none of them would share their secrets!

Concerned Elder: Now there are no secrets.

Right. **Millennials share everything**! The moment we figure anything out we post on social media, blog about it, write tutorials, or create online courses, (which can be extremely lucrative BTW).

Nowadays, any nine-year-old can look up diagrams of linear-optical-quantum computers, as they listen to a lecture on the brain's amygdala, in the background, while also playing games on their smart phone. And they do this effortlessly, while picking Trader Joes gummies out of their braces. Shout out to #TJchews...

This multi-channel input contributes to the Millennial's hatred of barriers and rigidity... as well as our distractibility.

Which leads me to our first major flaw....

MILLENNIAL FLAW #1: WE WANT EVERYTHING RIGHT NOW

We are so used to getting information quickly that when it's not there, it's annoying. We like our apps to work quickly, we want we want access over ownership; we want our services to integrate behind the scenes, and we want to get alerts when the taco truck is nearby. Everything needs to be faster with us, and that means constantly staying up to date.

It's good because we aren't as reticent to learn new skillsets as some of our parents. A Millennial isn't going to go thirty years and *not* pick up new computer skills. It's simply won't be an option for most of us.

When we start a project, we know that the knowledge, or tutorials, or the source files are out there. We just have to look. And we know it's just a matter of drilling down on a topic for a few hours to get up and running.

My friend Christoph, made his first interactive virtual reality project in two days! I was able to create a fully functioning online store that accepts credit cards and tracks shipments in about five hours.

MILLENNIAL FLAW #2: WE GET BORED QUICKLY AND ARE EASILY DISTRACTED...

The bad part of having so much access to new information all the time is that it's changing our cognition patterns. In fact, young people are more wired to remember *where* they find information, than *what* the information actually was. We are literally offloading our memories to technology. God help us if the power goes out...

Because smart phones are so damn good now, the internet is a pervasive opportunity for distraction. **Take it from me, constant distraction is definitely dangerous.** It affects our ability to focus by teaching our brains to expect a new dopamine source at a very rapid pace. Rather than to follow long chains of thought towards a deeper conclusion.

This can create so called, 'compulsion loops' whereby we automatically snag our phone every time we get a little bit bored. When trying to build long term memory storage, constant disruption is a problem. Especially in a world where, let's face it, we all have to learn stuff we aren't that interested in. Every time we interrupt ourselves studying that textbook, the cache of short term memory that we've built up has an opportunity to be overridden. Especially, if the new activity is more *stimulating*.... Like, um... watching gorgeous people making love to each other...

Staring at your math homework when an endless supply of amazing games, articles, Instagram posts, Tumblr feeds, pornography, and YouTube videos are calling to you is really freakin' hard sometimes. Partaking in too much distraction is like getting tackled every 2 minutes in a football game. After 2 hours, your brain doesn't feel very good.

Concerned Elder (My Friends Mom): Wait, wait, wait! You guys watch pornography on your phone!?

Uh, duuuhh.... The average kid starts watching porn at age eleven.

Concerned Elder: My gosh!

What? We're friends now, we can talk about this stuff right?

(This is an unfortunate segue way) …. but in the book *"Deep Work"* by Georgetown professor Cal Newport, he makes the case that the people who will be the most successful in the Information Age, ironically, will be the people who are the best at periodically shutting themselves off from it. He calls this, 'doing the deep work'. Diving head first into a specific subject, without distraction, for long periods of extended study.

And you know what? I think, he's right on the money. I highly recommend his book. I didn't finish it because I got distracted halfway through -- but *you* seem like the reading type. lol

The constant thirst for new distraction, is the single biggest obstacle standing in the Millennial's way. And it leads me to:

WHAT WE NEED MORE OF

We need more young people with the ability to delineate and explicate clear lanes of thought, without falling prey to groupthink. In other words, people who have laid the intellectual bricks THEMSELVES, in their own mind, to arrive at conclusion x,y, or z. People who don't settle for what they think they *should* say. People who have clear individuality and viewpoint, and aren't afraid to go against the grain if necessary.

I think we actually need *more* people who have spent huge amounts of time aimlessly sailing the informational ocean of the modern internet, coming out and talking about all the stuff they've learned with the intention to consolidate their findings via a unique Youtube channel, Twitch stream, or other avenue. I realize that's a huge challenge, because being an introverted researcher type person, usually means you're not the most social.

A perfect example is 21 one year old 'Masaman'. A demography and ethnography geek. His videos talk about little known periods in history, and the various ethnic interactions that have shaped people today. Basically Ancestry.com, on crack.

This is an incredibly touchy subject matter that he *SHOWING* people how to discuss, with respect and dignity, without the slightest bit of racism. We need more people doing this type of work. People who inject fascinating, but little known topics into the zeitgeist.

The real intellectual power players are going to be ones who have taken in TONS of stuff, and synthesized it in unique ways. Which takes a ton of personal fortitude and **private thinking time**. Which I don't think most Millenials/Gen Z'ers get enough of.

At the moment, we have so many communities circle-jerking each other. GroupThink is rampant. We need people more willing to cross the isle, so to speak. Not just in politics, but intellectually. Weaver together-ers. Bridge builders between all the established ideologies of society. Politically, scientifically, artistically, etc etc. And then we need those people to be entrepreneurial in their actions. And then the world will be a better place ☺

We need millennials who talk about modern issues in a more nuanced way - without relying on memes (which are a great, but are relatively low-rez form of communications).

This is why TED Talks are so popular, or great podcasts, and we need it times 10, as the mainstream media continues to stagnate and die. Wheew...

Even though I just got on my soapbox about the power of aimlessly wondering the internet... let me say that many Millennials *are* also aware of distraction-addiction,

So to combat this, many of us have very elaborate strategies for avoiding our cell phone at times. In fact my phone is currently in another room, behind a closed door, far away from my itchy fingers. My friend Steve, the deepest thinker I know, will go 48 hours without responding to a text. This is very annoying for party planning, but really awesome when you get him talking in the Jacuzzi.

You should also know that many kids give up videogames cold turkey, during their first or second year of college. (It's sort of a 21st century rite of passage). However, we pick it back up once our career has stabilized. Which is why the average gamer is actually thirty-three years old.

The dreaded feeling of being overstimulated is totally fatal if you let it get out of hand. It's literally a 'mode' your brain gets stuck in. I've had bouts of it. You'll write a few lines, then you'll get bored and grab your phone. When you're in this mode it's much harder to suppress urges of all kinds. You're more prone to over-eat.

What was supposed to be a thirty second Instagram break can easily turn into an hour. You don't feel satiated because you've temporarily trained your brain to expect its next little burst of new information.

I'll say it for you, Concerned Elder... it's bad. A few 30 minute social media or YouTube sessions in the morning can ruin a good day. Drawing, painting, (or writing the book that will let you escape your parent's house) becomes pretty much impossible.

Boredom > Curiosity > Distraction > Over Stimulation >Loss of Focus >
Depression Over Lost Productivity

Ironically, the best information on ways to combat this equation is found on the internet! (Life hack: take a nap, go for a walk, or meditate)

Concerned Elder (my mom): What the hell is a 'life hack'?

A life hack is any trick, or tip that helps you live a better life!

Mom: You mean advice?

Ya! But no one wants advice. It's more fun to get life hacks.

Mom: Okay, life hack your laundry, please.

...That's not how it's used...

I don't want to sugar coat this. **The abundance of distraction is going to cost a lot of Millennials their careers.** It's a real problem. It's gotten so bad, that a common form of procrastinating is to go on 'motivation binges'; watching hours of motivational speakers on YouTube but never actually *doing* anything. The irony is not lost on us...

All this being said, I'd rather face the possibility of being distracted by too much juicy stuff to see, hear, watch, and learn than not have access to anything outside of my village. Like, 99.999% of all humans that have ever lived.

With the good comes the bad, and like any new technology, best practices will evolve along with it.

A GENERATION OF CYBER EXPLORERS

Ok, onto the fun stuff. The internet gets a bad rap for being the home of endless pornography and stupid videos. And yes, there's a lot of both. But even the worst of it, I see as serving an important role towards global cohesion, as long we bring the correct mindset to it all.

Concerned Elder: Huh?

We are the first generation to have 24/7 access to a large swath of the human experience. Even if a lot of internet stuff is pure silliness or junk, it's something we all share. It's *our* junk.... humanity's junk, and we subconsciously look at it that way. We are the generation of explorers. Not explorers of unknown geography, but explorers of *each other....*

It all comes down to sheer exposure. **The amount of media we've absorbed through our eyeballs unites us in a way no other generation has been united.**

Everyone knows about Google, Wikipedia, Twitter, Tumblr, Instagram, Facebook, Snapchat, and Pinterest, and the big one, YouTube. But even media sharing sites like Tumblr, Reddit, ICanHAzCheeseburger, 9Gag, ImGUR, and WorldStarHipHop which tend to collect more 'low brow' video content, are playing a big role in transferring unedited, raw human experience from one person to another.

That's right, I think dance videos, prank videos, video blogs, men-wrestling-catfish-videos, Snapchats, and Lexington Steel videos (you can guess what industry he's in) are literally doing a service to mankind. It's giving each of us access to other people's way of life, no matter how different or shocking.

In fact that's the irony of it. The weirder something is, the *more* it's shared by others... Kids have been bombarded by fringe characters of all behaviors and 'sizes. We have had to internalize, and somehow cope with the diversity of the human experience from a much, much, earlier age. And that deeply effects a person's understanding of the human existence.

Here's the thing: each time you watch a video, your brain must instantly figure out the social context, personality type, status, and location of the people in them. Over the course of thousands and thousands of videos, this starts to create a general awareness of the scope of humanity and all the diverse flavors that it can take. The whole world is shrinking massively in this sense.

This means that Millennials/Gen Z have a more detailed mosaic of the human experience than other generations. Well actually, the internet is creating a mental construct of the world that's way better than a mosaic, because each tile represents video footage -- not just flat imagery.

We may not have as much particular knowledge as the older generations yet, but we've had a ton of exposure that will deepen any knowledge we attain.

Concerned Elder: ...Um ok...

So, it's become much harder to be completely insular these days; to hold onto small-minded beliefs. The internet creates a certain 'cultural relativism'. We can't help but see our own culture relative to the other possible models that are out there. And so people are becoming less culturally rigid, and more accepting. Which is a great thing in a racially diverse, globalized world. It doesn't mean Millennials don't judge each other, but this is a big step in an unfolding process towards a more open society.

What is the effect of this mass cultural exchange going to be 25 years from now? When we can send altered reality videos to each other in real time? When we can explore cities around the world in real time VR? This process has just begun! In fact Gen Z, or iGen as they are known, already relates more to the notion of 'global citizenship' than nationalism. And they're like thirteen!? 58% of adults thirty-five and older agree that "kids today have more in common with their global peers than they do with adults in their own country". That's shocking.

What I'm talking about is very similar to the effect of traveling. Except youngsters are traveling all around the globe through our phones every single day. When your friend sends you a link, it could *literally* take you anywhere. We have access to experts and idiots from around the world, and we often watch both consecutively with just a few swipes in between. Our default mental state *has to be* fairly open. It's the only way to stay sane.

Even if many of the dumber viral videos have somewhat of a voyeuristic, 'check this out' vibe, they still spark all of the same **meta-analysis** that our brains do subconsciously.

These are fundamental upgrades to the human experience that have shaped how Millennials approach the world in a deep-seated way.

INTERNET VIDEOS AND EMOTIONAL INTELLIGENCE

Surfing the internet is practically everyone's favorite hobby. Why? Because it's hard wired into our primal brains to seek out novel information. If there's one thing Millennials are best at, it's digging up silly, absurd and random content from the underbelly of the internet. Many of our concerned elders worry that this is a total waste of time. But I want to make a detailed argument that they are totally wrong. Because, even the stupidest videos raise EQ, or emotional intelligence quotient.

Here's a formula I have developed.

Early Exposure = Intuitive Tolerance

It states that when you are exposed to something early enough, you become intuitively accepting of it. Children are born curious and loving… until they are taught differently by an unfortunate incident.

I've seen people tripping, pranking, preaching, wing-suiting, exploring, spelunking, crying, hunting, crashing, dancing, eating, and laughing on all seven continents. I've seen rich kids fall into luxurious pools and scream about their ruined phone, and I've seen people falling off of the roofs of their favelas with a smile on their face.

I've listened to real drug dealers talk slang in the 'trap', and plastic surgery addicts explain their latest procedures. And of course, we've watched plenty of fairly normal people every day on Snapchat.

Internet videos are a display of the entire gamut of human experience. Hence

Christoph's description, 'faucet of exposure'.

EQ, or 'emotional intelligence quotient', is the ability to recognize your own emotions and the ability to recognize and empathize with the emotions of others. It's very much in demand these days. The World Economic Forum's Future of Jobs Report states that high EQ will be one of the top ten job requirements by 2020. In a Career Builder Survey, 71% of hiring managers said they value EQ over IQ. In fact, EQ training is now a blossoming field.

Successful CEO and Tech Investor Gary Vaynerchuck puts it like this: "As IQ based tasks are being commoditized, (by computers), EQ is becoming more and more important."

Well, the internet is the perfect tool for the growth of this critical aspect of the human psyche, and it's doing it very much behind the scenes.

One of the recognized forms of growing your emotional intelligence is observing and interacting with other people. Well, it just so happens the life of the Millennial is a constant stream of minimally curated media, rants and comments sections.

Comment sections are always a mixed bag... they can be brilliant, hilarious or horribly rude. Sometimes they are all three, but they never fail to be interesting. Typically, we watch a video, and then we immediately check to see how many other people feel the same way we do.

Concerned Elder: Why?

Because it's fun. It's not uncommon to see ten or eleven radically different opinions on the same video. Sometimes out of twenty comments, there'll be one that just nails your exact feelings better than you could say it yourself. All of this builds EQ because it's making us interface with other people's ideas each day and it's happening organically.

From the very popular 'unboxing videos' --

Concerned Elder:?????? Wait. What?

You buy something and open it, and react on camera...duhhhhhhh

-- to video diary 'vlogs' to 'cringe videos' to all sorts of compilation videos, like '10 Insane Things People Do', to picture memes, to Snapchat stories, Instagram posts, online news articles... All of these forms of content expose us to what other people are doing and thinking.

This unprecedented access to each other has created an emotional 'default' setting that is more socially open and conscious. In fact, I would say our generation has a heightened understanding of the term *human experience*. At the very least, a more visceral one.

Also keep in mind, the internet is not just connecting Americans, it's connecting rest of the world. And it's doing it quickly in small entertaining bites.

Granted, I'm a little biased on this topic of exposure because one of my favorite things to do, being an artist, is to actively explore highly exotic cultures. Did you know the people of Kau, in South Sudan, have a word for every single body position a human can possibly make?

I've watched documentaries on the pygmies of West Africa and the Mandari tribe of Eastern African; on the Mongolian throat singers who drink fermented horse milk, and the Amazonian shamans. There's probably an as yet unexplained phenomenon of the brain that occurs when you watch a Dinka tribal dance followed immediately by a documentary on Malaysian sweatshop workers followed by some kid in Idaho doing a flamboyant 'happy dance' because he got an 'A' on a test, immediately followed by a dude in in the Faroe Islands hunting false-killer whales to feed his family.

It's bizaare, interesting, scary, funny, logical, and irrational all at the same time. Kinda of like life right?

To me, the internet is like my little airplane, where I can fly all over the world and get a glimpse of how other people live.

Concerned Elder: Wow Dario, *you* must be a very special young man… but don't most kids your age just watch stupid stuff?

Thanks C.E. I appreciate your kind words. Stupid stuff like this?

EXCUSE ME...

The answer is yes.

Ultimate Fails Compilation 2016: Part 1 (December 2016) || FailArmy

3:15 / 17:07

    Take this funny video of a reporter getting spit on by a llama, while standing next to a traditional Peruvian woman. I got this from a 'fail video' compilation of funny accidents that people send in from all around the world. This single compilation spans many different countries. This was a viral sensation:

This is one of the last uncontacted tribes in the Amazon. Obviously, someone Photoshopped the Obama campaign signs. This is a perfect example of what I'm talking about. It's literally a joke *about* culture, made possible by the internet. It was just as funny freshman year as it is now.

Concerned Elder: If you wanna learn about other cultures, read a book, subscribe to National Geographic. Here's a thought, *actually* travel for goodness sakes. Talk to *actual* people. It seems like everything you guys intake is a fragmented, context-less mess of stuff!

Sorry if I'm annoying you, Concerned Elder. You're right. Most of it is totally devoid of context. That's the beauty and the downfall of the internet. I'm not making the case that this 'soup of stuff' is the best way to learn or experience anything. A lot of it is silly and ephemeral. But like it or not, everyone my age has participated in it.

Anything that is ubiquitous is powerful. I'm simply trying to point that out. While this style of interaction and exposure is imperfect, it's still doing *something*. It's creating an international flow of stuff that is beginning to integrate everyone in a way that has never happened before in history. So although I totally agree with you Mr. Elder, it's not *quite* as trivial as you might think.

Disclaimer: For all of my Millennial readers, for whom all of this is brutally obvious, feel free to skim the next few sections. If you're still skeptical of the mystical/ transformative power of the internet, then keep reading.

Let's take this one famous video from India of a tiger leaping out of the reeds, twelve feet in the air, and biting a man who is riding an elephant. The video ends by showing his bloody arm and shocked face. On the surface, it's horrifying. But if you break it down, there's quite a bit of information subliminally entering your brain.

Here is the link: https://www.youtube.com/watch?v=M4t0aeTX954

Click on it. Oops, this is paper... I forgot...

Let's do a very simple, breakdown of what your brain is processing:

A Case Study: Anatomy of a Tiger Attacking a Man Video...

1: If you didn't know it already, you learn that some people ride on giant leathery animals for transportation. AWESOME!

2: You witness the immense agility and strength of big cats. It's shocking to witness an adult tiger leap twelve feet into the air.

3: Then you think, "Wow, other people live under the threat of being EATEN -- by giant striped monsters." And then if you're thankful, you say, "I'm pretty darn lucky to live where I live."

Now, as random as this example is, if you've never seen any of this, you have just learned quite a lot. I was about thirteen when I saw this video.

All of the majesty of Nature is wrapped up in that thirty-second clip--both it's violent side and it's immense beauty. The vicious precision of the tiger and the sites and sounds of a mangrove forest, foreign to a Western mind. You also get to see how the man handles his gnarly injury. He's not panicking, but he's definitely in shock.

I came away with a deep respect for tigers, and also a curiosity for rural India, which I've since taken some time to learn more about. **I do not think videos like these should be underestimated in their ability to influence consciousness. (Especially when you watch TONS of them everyday).**

THE IMMENSE POWER OF THE SPIN-OFF SEARCH

All of this internet exploring is taken to a new level by **the power of the spin-off search**. We've all had the experience of seeing something awesome online and quickly googling it to find out more. What does a decade of random internet content *and* spin off searches do to someone?

Random Videos + Spin Off Searches = A ton of exposure to people and ideas.

This is where the real **positive benefits of stupid videos** lie. When you see something so shocking, so appalling, so funny, so different that it compels you to do actual research about the topic. **This how kids find their passion nowadays.**

Let's consider what the spin off searches of the tiger video could be if someone is inquisitive.

I remember googling 'tigers' to see some more. After a few seconds of clicking around, seeing images of tigers hunting, pouncing, prancing, sleeping, swimming, looking adorable, performing in Vegas, roaring, eating a deer leg etc., I skimmed an article about the tiger sanctuaries of India. I quickly learned just how endangered they are. Less then 3,200 left in the wild. I got sad ☹. I clicked the back-button on my browser to run from my sadness.

I then saw pictures of baby tigers and white tigers, and giant Ligers the size of ponies. I clicked on a tiger hiding in the snow. I learned that tigers still lived in Siberia. Where's Siberia again?

I opened a new window, typed 'siberia' and sixty pictures of maps popped up. I learned that Siberia is actually in South-Eastern Russia. Pretty far from India where the rest of the population is found. I typed in 'tiger population map' and saw that their 'historic-range' used to extend much farther north.

While doing this, I couldn't help but pick up on the locations of Mongolia, Kazakhstan, Uzbekistan, and whah..? Russia shares a slight border with North Korea? I had no idea. And half of Russia sits on top of China? I always thought they were next to each other. I quickly realized how flawed my sense of geography was.

I closed the map...back to Google images. There's that gigantic Liger again. I need to get back to my drawings, but I *have* to click on *that*. Now, all of the sudden, I'm reading about genetics, phenotypes, dominant and recessive genes etc. I learned how *in vitro* fertilization is used. I learned that if there's a tiger mother and lion father, then the resulting Liger will be enormous...

Ok, enough with tigers, what is *in vitro* fertilization? Blah blah, blah...

Then I googled elephants! Did you know that Indian elephants can grow up to twelve feet tall and weigh blah blah blah...You get the point, and I'm exhausted from typing this all out. I won't deprive you of your own fun.

We've just taken a stroll through anthropology, conservation, geology, and genetics in a few minutes. And to the kid falling down these rabbit holes -- it feels like **exploration**, not **'studying'**. Isn't this a better way to spark interest in new things than having it force fed?

Imagine doing similar jaunts, a dozen times a day, for nearly a decade and a half. You can imagine the sheer volume of topics and imagery one sifts through. Now admittedly, not all of it is stored. But it starts to create a **fabric of familiarity** just like anything else in life. Virtually every Millennial has kept up this practice to some extent. In fact you can bet on it. Why? Because contrary to the programming that high school implants in you: learning is actually fun, when *your* guiding it.

Through this random exploration, a kid could discover they have a passion for tiger conservation, or genetically engineering big cats, or some other obscure career path.

It's better to get excited about a subject, and live in that excitement for a

while, before you dive into the drier parts through school, through college, etc. It shouldn't be the other way around.

Millennial's are infamous for their ability to 'waste time'. In her 2017 Ted Talk, marketer and media expert Baily Parnell stated the we spend 2-3 hours on social media per day and 11.5 hours using technology.

Most people would say that's a lot of wasted time. I say that's a lot of data collection. All of it *isn't* going to be substantial. But the more shit you've seen the more curious you are, and the more types of people you have had the chance to observe.

THE INTERNET DOESN'T BUILD EMPATHY, BUT IT PAVES THE WAY

The power of the internet to initiate empathy is tremendous. People who disagree with this are overthinking it. Do you know what Kowloon city looks like in China? My friend Steve sent me this in 9th grade.

In 9th grade I learned that I could have been born here ^

...and one of these could be my home. ^

As cognitive neuroscientist Katri Saarikivi states, "Empathy comes from all of the tools we have to understand other". She goes on to say that the best way to build empathy is to become an explorer of the world. Well, most Millennials have done that. A LOT of that. Let us remember that the fear of the unknown is the source of all prejudice. Fear leads to the 'us vs them' mentality, and the *loss* of empathy for other people.

If you want to get all computer science-ey, the internet is literally letting us mind map the rest of the world, bit by bit. And it's really fun to do!

Concerned Elder: Give me a break. You can't possibly understand other people's lives without physically being there and talking to them.

And I partially agree. I'm not saying watching minimally produced videos is *as* good as visiting India, or Kowloon City yourself. I'm just saying it's a whole lot better than nothing. It's putting us into contact with lifestyles, voices and faces we would never see or hear otherwise.

All of this digital traveling is inspiring us to *actually* travel more. Millennials are 23% more likely to travel abroad than previous generations. According to Hospitality.net we are on pace to spend 1.4 trillion (!) on travel by 2020.

And the Millennial traveler has very different tastes than our older brethren. "The trademark of the Boomer was that they wanted familiarity, safety, and comfort," according to Wolfgang Lindlbauer, chief leader of Global Operations at Marriott International. "We have found that the next generation wants the exact opposite of what we are delivering."

Millennials want to experience local culture; we want stories, not souvenirs. We are choosing to stay at places that have strong local connections, and which ideally, support local businesses and customs. We don't want to look at it through our hotel windows. Why? Because we've seen the world on our phone-windows and now we want to experience it.

Earth is now like a massive ant colony except each ant has access to videos of what all the other ants are doing. Empathy goes hand in hand with this process. And if it doesn't you're a total prick. I'm sorry, but it's the truth. If observing people doesn't make you feel something/relate to them, then you've got bigger problems to solve.

WHAT ABOUT YO' GRANDMA?

Let me ask you -- how was my grandmother supposed to have this volume of 'input' circa 1935 in Gary Indiana?

I feel bad for my grandma, but my grandkids will probably be mocking me. They will be hopping into each other's virtual worlds. They will be able to visit India through cameras that can record 3d information. They will have completely immersive, real-time, virtual reality tiger experiences. Their schools will host VR live-streams with Indian schools. They will have videogames where you can visualize the Hindu Loca's, supposed realms of heaven, made of different geometric structures. They will have interactive 360 degree reporting from around the world. They will laugh at the mere morsels we consume.

PEOPLE ARE FINDING THEIR PASSIONS THROUGH THE INTERNET

Finding your passion is largely a numbers game. It's about how many topics you've come across, and how much they caught your interest, and how much you've researched them. The internet has given us a wide net that we can cast upon the world. It is insuring that we all have a better chance at finding what we are *really* interested in.

Concerned Elder: Aren't we developing a bunch of dilettantes who only know a little about a lot of things?

Yes, that's a danger, as I mentioned earlier… but…the French philosopher and physicist Blaise Pascal wrote, "Since we cannot know all that there is to be known about anything, we ought to know a little about everything."

Thanks Blaise. I totally agree. Knowing a little about a lot is all most people get from school anyway. I don't remember 75% of the explicit information I was taught. I just remember broad fields that interested me. And I remember 0% of anything related to calculus because my teacher was so horrible.

It's better to have a population that's been exposed to a TON of stuff because statistically, more people will discover the one or two things that cause them do the 'deep-work' as Cal Newport calls it. This is the sifting through the tiny little mechanics: the work that requires a person to actually want to turn off their cellphone for hours at a time. (You have to be pretty interested in a subject to do that!)

People only learn deeply when they really care about a subject, which comes from being inspired by someone you look up to.

This is how I, a teenage basketball player, first got interested in art. I loved video games, and was constantly admiring the graphics that kept getting better each year. So, I started going to sites dedicated to the 'behind the scenes' of games. I found an obscure forum post discussing how the characters were designed. That's when I discovered a digital sculpting program called Zbrush, by developer Pixologic, which allows the user to sculpt characters on of the computer. You know, like Gollum, or the people from Avatar.

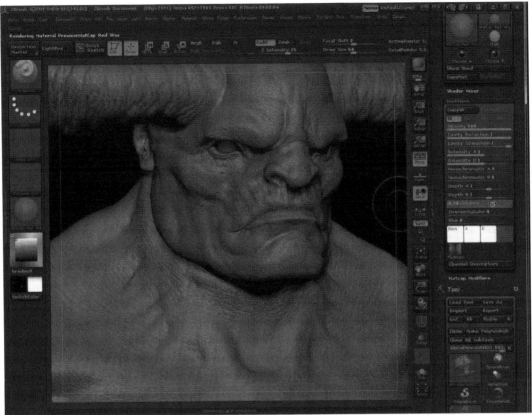

(Art by Scott Spencer)

The tool was very complex and intimidating at first. But I saw the work of the experts and was so amazed. I had so much darn enthusiasm for figuring out how they did it.

With every ounce of my little fourteen-year old soul, I *had* to learn:

1: What every single button of the program did (over 200 buttons)

2: How to sculpt human anatomy

3: How to sculpt animal anatomy; noses, trunks, claws, hair, ears, etc.

4: How to stylize when you sculpt. A very deep subject.

And that's how I discovered one of my favorite hobbies in high school. I was a strange mix of jock and weirdo art-guy who sculpts aliens after I did my homework. (Most of the time, *before* I did my homework). In order to improve, I had to look at tutorials and study the techniques of the old master artists. So I started looking at the work of Michelangelo, Bernini and ancient Greek sculptors.

In order to fully understand their work, I felt obliged to learn about their beliefs, and their worldviews. I started to learn about 'humanism' and idealism as philosophies. And on and on down the art rabbit hole I traveled. And the key is that I *wanted* to do all of this because I loved the art I saw online. No one was making me. And even knowing my passion, I still picked the wrong college at first! (But that's another chapter....)

And this entire field of interest all started from getting hooked on some really silly videogames when I was five. Like Crash Bandicoot, where you play a genetically engineered rodent. Or my favorite, Spyro: The Dragon. Where, as a cute purple dragon, you explore magical realms in the clouds, collecting colorful emeralds. That's where the **power of silly content** can lead!

This ^

Can lead to studying this^ Which can lead to writing a book summarizing and critiquing the Zeitgeist of my entire generation. Duh... ☺

The punchline to the story, is that Zbrush has since grown into an immensely versatile, industry standard software package servicing 4 different industries. Accidentally learning it young kid, was a gift from the career gods. (Kids: grow up with your software!)

We now have a global infrastructure in place to follow our curiosities on a whim. **To learn by procrastinating, and procrastinate by learning.**

RACISM, HATRED AND THE INTERNET: AN OPTIMISTIC POINT OF VIEW

It will be really hard for people of my generation to live in a self-contained bubble. The ultra wealthy and powerful can't hide out in their mansions and pretend the rest of the world doesn't exist anymore. The 'evil CEO stereotype' will loose traction. The Millennial corporate executive of the future will be a different entity. They will have an innate level of social awareness having grown up on Snapchat, Facebook, YouTube Instagram, and having *seen* the areas of the world that their actions are affecting. Watching people expressing themselves in a genuine form, every single day cultivates tolerance, curiosity, and yes, empathy if you're not a dickhead. Remember, Early Exposure = Intuitive Tolerance!

We've already seen how the viral ability of videos to spread has exposed tremendous injustices, illegal arrests, tragic shootings... And it's affecting public policy.

Concerned Elder: What about people who use the internet to spread hatred?

Let me acknowledge that a small number of young, depressed, disenfranchised people are being radicalized on the internet. It's insidious. It's gross.

Of course there are people who use the internet to find the worst in others. People who make hateful comments on videos so the rest of us have to read it. These are called 'trolls', by the way. Others seek to justify their racists beliefs by searching for the very worst aspects in other cultures through the internet. These are a tiny fraction of internet users, who make up a large fraction of the comment section and news headlines. So we are a given a false impression of their size and effect on society. **If there's any curing these people, it's going to be the knowledge and exposure to other viewpoints that blows the lid off of their insular beliefs. And for those who are severely disenfranchised, the internet is the best place to seek new ideas, new principles, hope, guidance etc.**

I once saw a video of a white supremacist enjoying a Japanese videogame, with Mexican food sitting on the table behind him. If this guy can't see the irony in his life, then I'm not sure he can be helped.

These people are missing a critical piece of enlightenment that the internet can give them. They are failing to see that within all the varying cultures are the shared emotions of humanity. We just express them through different cultural archetypes. At least that's the lesson I've gotten out of the internet.

They are also missing a big lesson: that there isn't any supreme or 'superior culture'.

A Brief Lesson on Cultural Diversity From A 24-Year Old White Male

Cultures are a reflection of group priorities. So if a certain group of people have certain tendencies, it's simply because they prioritize those over others.

As we learned from Darwin, environmental factors have shaped our physical variations as humans. But they also shape what building materials a culture has access to historically. Which in turn, affects a culture's priorities.

It's an invalid argument to say any one behavior is better than another. There are only behaviors that serve different goals.

So, for instance, in the West, we deem something to be *worth* doing if it yields possessions. Social status is generally given to those with money and influence over other people. But how do you quantify spiritual wealth? How to do you quantify connectedness to community and to spirit? These are values that many of the 'poorest' people have in spades, and have solidified into elaborate ritual practices, just as we have quantified our priorities into elaborate practices.

In indigenous Amazonia, drinking a hallucinogenic Ayahuasca brew and spending eight hours on a psychedelic vision quest is considered entirely practical. Does it lead to possessions? Not directly.

Who is right?

If the goal is to place spiritual well-being at the forefront of how we structure society, then we are failing miserably. But the Amazonians are 'wrong' if their goal is to build skyscrapers, go to the moon, etc.

As humans, we are in a constant process of exchanging our ideas and integrating new ones. So this is why racial arguments, cultural superiority arguments, and sexuality comparisons are frankly, really silly. They are just different sets of priorities that different groups have – **and it's always evolving.**

This is why the internet is great! It's the new medium by which the world shares cultural ideas.

BUT WE CAN MIX AND MATCH IDEAS

The internet is giving the entire world the chance to figure out which group is doing something that could be of value to rest of us. Underneath all of the food pics, and selfies, and occasional racism, this is what it's actually doing.

So, for instance, Ayahuasca is now gaining popularity in America. According to a New Yorker article, more than one hundred Ayahuasca circles can be found on any given day in Manhattan. People are also traveling to the Amazon in droves to, as former CNN reporter Amber Lyon puts it, "...have every molecule of your body cleansed". Okay, those Amazonians might be onto something there --and America is now adopting it.

On a bigger scale, the Western influence on Chinese entertainment, business, and fashion has been profound. Okay, those Americans might be on to something... The African influence on American music, fashion, acting, comedy and language has been huge. Okay, so they're onto something good there...

The scientific study of idea transfer is called *memetics*. The smallest unit of an idea, is a 'meme'. Groups of memes combine to create our cultures, just like groups of genes create our bodies. (This is different than the *picture-memes* you find online. I'll get to those in the social media section.)

So what the internet is doing is it's letting everyone's cultural memes be accessible to everyone else. May the best memes win.

In some cases, memes directly compete with each other: using a fork vs. using chopsticks. In many cases, memes merge and combine to create new memes that are better tailored to the new environment. Jazz would be an example of a combined meme; Western instruments playing with an African rhythmic style.

Memes are a wonderful way to interpret history. For instance, China, for a majority of their history, has been very weary of the outside world. That was the prevailing 'meme', or behavior, on that subject. But because of that, the last hundred years have been tumultuous for them, as they try to adopt new ideas or memes to 'catch up' with Western memes that they now value as a culture.

So while you can't say any meme is '*better*' than another, memes do have opportunity cost. As ideas of all kinds travel around the world, the 'best ones' will rise to the top and become accepted. And by best, I just mean, those ideas which fill a perceived need.

And yes, bold faced aggression and imperialism has played a role in meme-spreading. Less nowadays the it used too...

It could well be, that in 1000 years, our ancestors will look back at this time period as simply 'the balancing of the worlds economic, religious, and scientific memes via the influence of a global cyber space'.

Meditation, an Eastern meme, is helping hundreds of millions of people worldwide, process their own thoughts better.

Ayahuasca, of the South American tradition, could be just the meme Western people need to recover from our overly stressed way of life.

Rap music, can now be found in nearly every country and language...

This is how humans work. We share our ideas and we find the best ones in all the key areas of life. First it was fire, the wheel, then farming, and now the internet. That's what we've done our entire history.

Okay, before we move on to social media, I would be remiss if I didn't touch upon....

INTERNET PORNOGRAPHY (*dun dun dun*)

Concerned Elder: So far, you're making the internet sound less harmful than I thought. But *how* are you going to defend porn?

Fake answer: Where are you supposed to learn all your moves?

Real Answer: Globally, we aren't hiding our bodies from each other anymore.

Everyone under forty has seen 'members' of every single race and cultural group having sex. As you can probably tell, I'm a big fan of not hiding stuff from each other.

In fact, there's an internet term called **Rule 32**. It goes like this: 'If you can think of a type of porn, it already exists'. And through some rigorous tests I performed in 9th grade -- that rule has yet to be proven wrong. That's right... *'A Maori Tribesman and Three Danish Men,'* is a real video. *'Off-Road ATV Bang Session in Forest'* exists. *'Swedish Couple Does It On A Frozen Lake Before Ice Breaks'* exists and has 100,000 views.

People my age have all seen so many penii, so many vaginae', and sooo many other strange things that I will shield you from. **And it's not because we're all perverts. It's just what you stumble upon as a kid with an internet connection.**

Concerned Elder: But surely this must effect a young brain!?

What does growing up with instant access to sexual imagery at the touch of a button do to a person? First, it fascinates / horrifies you. Secondly, it's devastating to your productivity. Then, hopefully it teaches you about discipline. **Porn is THE single biggest source of distraction for the Millennial male. PERIOD.**

It typically goes like this: you discover porn around 11 or 12 years old. It was probably an accident. On the internet, things can go from 0-100 pretty quickly.

As Christoph explains: "My first computer memory was when I was a little kid. My sister was on Girls.com, which was a digital companion site for American Girl Dolls. It had flash games, journals, interactive stuff, etc. So the timer goes off marking the end of her allotted computer time, I hop on, and go to Boys.com. It was gay porn. I was... I don't know how old? 1st or 2nd grade? I started crying and ran to my parents."

Porn starts as more of an odd curiosity than anything else. A Pandora's box of stuff you didn't know humans were capable of... and it's just a few wrong clicks away. Slowly, you grow more familiar with it. As puberty starts to kick in, you start to figure out what you like and what you don't like. Your friends are most likely going through the same 'exploration' process, so it can be fun to prank each other with absurd stuff. You might be chatting online, or texting, and your friend says, 'check this out!' You click it, only to find a woman sticking an octopus up her vagina. Or worse...

This is the 'ready for anything at any time' attitude that the Millennial 7th grade boy had to develop with his friends. These pranks were the engine behind the 'Two Girls One Cup' phenomenon when I was in high school. It was video of girls pooping in a cup... and doing other stuff. But it was hilarious to watch your friends writhe in a combination of laughter and horror as they watched it. Kids would watch it in big groups and record themselves. Ahh... good times...

Concerned Elder: Oh, Lord help us...

There are other shock videos that you must never watch. '*LemonParty*', or '*BME Pain Olympics*', '*Goatse*' and others.

You know that one messy cry that you shared with your best friend that bonded you for life? That's what some porn is to kids. The more you're scarred by watching something truly gross, the more you laugh about it years later. My friends and I all look back on these adolescent porn adventures with fond memories. Personally, I don't think they did *that* much harm...But it does open your mind at early an age.

The mental framework you used to contextualize porn says a lot about you. Some kids get super involved in the psychology of different sexual desires at an early age, and would read clinical articles about that. I didn't care about that point view for whatever reason, preferring to stay an objective observer. I took a biologist's approach to the weirdness. I remembering comparing shapes of penis' mushrooms, and the parts of vaginas to flowering plants. (Not that weird if you think about it.)

As as you get older, porn starts to actually be used for what it's meant for. Fantasy fulfillment. Good ol' regular porn is also educational for many kids with conservative parents. So, my fake answer wasn't actually so fake.

As my friend Billy says:

"I had some crazy ideas about how sex worked when I was kid. Like, I thought dicks grew out of vaginas, and the more sperm you put in a girl the more kids she'd have." Porn is the main source of 'Advanced Sex Ed' for most kids beyond the overly purified facts that we got in school.

Most boys spend the summer of 8th grade in a hormone driven masturbatory stupor. Three, four, five times in a day is something many teens attempt at least a few times. Parents: when your child starts producing an awful lot of laundry– now you know why.

The frequent porn use of middle-school boys led to an interesting experience that many guys my age had to navigate when we started dating real women -- I mean girls.

We had already a few years of looking at grown-up women doing very grown-up things. We found there was somewhat of an astronomical gap between the sexual education and expectations of boys, versus that of the girls. But this might actually be an outdated statement. Because 7 years ago, when I was in the middle of high school, girls watched notably less porn than they do now. Nowadays, something like 90% of boys

11-18 have used porn and between 30-60% of girls. Though in these studies it's often hard to distinguish between 'exposure to porn' and the regular 'use' of it.

As we get older, the numbers stay pretty consistent. 80-90% of men age 18-29 are watching porn at least once a month based on studies by the American Psychological Association and the Barna Group; and its somewhere between 30% and 50% of women.   But even if women are watching more porn now, they tend to want different things out of it. Women tend to watch porn that is more tender and sensual.

They gravitate toward scenes that spend time on the emotional content, not just the interlocking parts. Interestingly, straight women tend to watch lesbian porn at much higher rates. Also, porn tends to not be so addicting as it is for men.

Many young men are overdoing it these days. Something between 10% and 20% of men admit to being addicted, according to various studies. With another 10-20% who 'wish they watched less'. This is millions of people...

One of the negative repercussions regarding the use of pornography is that it's causing some men to skimp on the intimacy and expect rougher sex right off the bat. As researcher Dr Struthers of the University of Chicago puts it, "Sex is turning into masturbation rather than being part of a process of intimacy with another person. As we fall deeper into the mental habit of fixating on [pornographic images] neural pathways are created that set the course for the next time an erotic image is viewed. Over time these neural paths become wider as they are repeatedly traveled with each exposure to pornography. They become the automatic pathway through which interactions with woman are routed."

The implication being that your nude partner is being interpreted as merely the visual stimulus that will allow you to achieve orgasm, rather than as a real-life person with whom to emotionally connect with.

And like our videogames and our marijuana -- porn has gotten a hell of a lot better lately. A lot of it is very cinematic and many of the adult-actresses look like supermodels nowadays.

Porn is a particularly bad thing to overuse because sexual pleasure is one of the most deeply embedded pleasure centers. Sex quite literally is a drug! The chemical cocktail that it creates in our brains is potent, and can lead to withdrawal symptoms when you over do it too long.

Over-using it for days on end creates a malaise, or a brain fog between 'high's' that many of us have experienced at one point or another. Your motivation drops, and you become an all-round less clear-headed person. The only thing that excites you, is more porn. If this goes on for too long, self-esteem begins to drop and a disconnect within yourself can occur. Self loathing. Depression.... Your actions aren't matching the person you know you are. *No bueno...*

You can take it to the bank, that every Millennial male you know, has gone too far down the porn rabbit hole at one time or another. Having read many testimonials online from people trying to stop, here is the progression that seems to occur.

Step 1: The Boredom Factor. Mobile porn can quickly become your go-to activity when you're simply bored. It's just too damn easy. And everything you need to get started is in your pants. Just like social media can cause compulsion loops, so can porn. Because it's constantly updating.

Step 2: A Mental Crutch. Things can quickly it can go from boredom activity to an on demand mental escape vector; an intense ten-minute getaway from life's problems. The average user on Pornhub stays for nine minutes and thirty seconds. You're in this phase, when you say to yourself, 'I'll jerk off, and then I'll do my work'. But of course, after you indulge yourself, you don't feel like doing anything. This stage is precarious because what you're really doing is taking all of your healthy excitement towards being productive, and wasting it on porn. This is how porn slowly sucks the life out of you.

Step 3: Full-blown addiction. The constant accessibility starts to win out over your other daily activities. As you use porn more over the course of weeks, your sensitivity to these neurotransmitters can get reduced. So it's the classic addictive cycle, where you're constantly chasing that big buzz, but not giving your brain enough time to rest. If you're at this state, you've probably been neglecting other aspects of your life which can add to feelings of depression and desire to escape.

On the extreme end of the spectrum—porn can make you disinterested in having sex with real people. Why 'suffer' through all the cultural formalities of dating, when my greatest fantasy is... one sec... it's bookmarked right here. Boom. You get the point.

As was featured in a Time magazine cover story, porn-induced-erectile dysfunction or P.I.E.D. as it's called, is a real thing for hundreds of thousands of otherwise healthy young men. This is caused when a real partner, can't excite you as much as pornography.

Concerned Elder: The cure is obvious. Stop watching porn!

But that's like telling an alcoholic to not drink when a fifth of vodka is always in his pocket.

Earlier, I said that Millennials were test subjects, right? Well, the results are in: Overly frequent porn use is extremely disruptive to a person's emotional well-being.

PORNO-HOLICS ANONYMOUS

As a result of this silent epidemic, many great online communities have sprung up centered around quitting porn. Along the lines of AA. There are forums where people post each day on their struggles with quitting. Other members give them encouragement. It's really cool, actually. People write inspiring testimonials of how amazing they feel having quit for x amount of time. These people act as encouragement for others still in the struggle. There are 30 day, 60 day, and 90 day 'challenges' people try to complete. (90 days is supposedly what it takes to fully rejuvenate your brain from heavy usage).

I don't want to be a total Debby-Downer on porn, though. I love that there's an uncensored plethora of material that contains humanity's most glorious physical specimens -- and our most gross impulses. In some weird, pyscho-social way, I think it's important for that to exist.

I'm sure you don't need a 24 year old to tell you that porn helps a lot of people. People who are disabled, severe introverts, people in sexless marriages, or just simply healthy young people who are focusing on their career and don't want to deal with finding a significant other at the moment. And I don't think it's necessary to *completely* abstain from it to be a functioning human. I view it just the same as alcohol, or chocolate cookies. It's a treat, until you mistreat it.

MILLENNIAL DATING HABITS

Despite our fancy dating apps Tinder, Grindr, Bumble, Down, Zoosk— *most* Millennials have actually had *fewer* sexual partners than Baby Boomers did. According to the General Social Survey by the University of Chicago, (and adjusting for age), Millennials have 8.26 sexual partners compared to 11.62 by the boomers. In fact 15% of Millennial girls 20 to 24 have not had sex since coming of age; also a higher percentage than baby-boomers. But interestingly, Millennials are much more accepting of premarital sex than our parents were at the ages of 18-29: 62% compared to just 47% of Baby Boomers. And a whopping 71% of Millennials are supportive of same-sex marriage.

When we do 'get it on', - we are more likely to engage in 'casual sex'. Which is defined as sex with someone whom we don't consider our 'bf' or 'gf'.

Some of this could be semantics though. Perhaps we don't go through the triviality of declaring each other 'boyfriend and girlfriend' for a week before we have sex. We prefer 'Friends with Benefits' as Gen Xers would call it, or 'hook up' culture as Millennials say.

Some have pinned the decrease in sexual activity to online dating apps and increasing obesity. Jean Twenge, author of the 2015 and 2016 University of Chicago studies of Millennial dating says, "It ends up putting a lot of importance on physical appearance, and that, I think, is leaving out a large section of the population. For a lot of folks who are of average appearance, marriage and stable relationships was where they were having sex ... [and dating apps may be] leaving some people with fewer choices more reluctant to search for partners at all."

Perhaps the decrease in the number of partners could be that we are more stressed than ever by academic and career pursuits. "It's a highly motivated, ambitious generation. A lot of them are afraid that they'll get into something they can't get out of, and they won't be able to get back to their desk and keep studying," says Helen Fisher, an anthropologist at Rutgers.

After doing my own exhaustive poll amongst my friends, I think increased awareness of STD's is also a factor. Something that was instilled in me through a gruesome slide show that I had to endure in high school. As well as numerous text message pranks performed on me by my friends. Have you seen blue muffin disease? Please, please, please don't look up blue muffin disease.

When you consider that Millennials are delaying marriage, the decrease in partners is even more curious. The average Millennial woman nowadays isn't getting married until age 29. But it's easy to see why. When we're living with our parents for longer and longer, we're strapped with student loans and unsure of finding a stable job -- marriage is very far down the agenda.

Personally, I'm not even thinking about marriage till I'm 39.5 years old. And children till I'm at least in my forties.

Concerned Elder (Mom): NOOOOOOOOO!

Mom, stay out of my book! Don't be a helicopter parent.

MAYBE IT'S A CONFIDENCE ISSUE?

The reluctance to go on the hunt for a partner is being reinforced by the millions of unrealistic expectations that the media and pornography feed us. **Body issues are a big subject of anxiety for many Millennials**. Many female models are now advocating against the use of Photoshop in an effort to try to fight unreasonable beauty standards. Men can be equally disheartened by comparing themselves to professional athletes and porn actors who obviously have—ahem-- 'excessive' physical traits. This can lead to 'body dysmorphia' or a compulsion to obsess over one's physical flaws.

Perhaps an increasing percentage of people are deeming themselves unattractive, and aren't pursuing relationships at all. There is a large subculture of this in

Japan. (FYI I learned that from a YouTuber. This is how we learn new things...)

I also think many of us are satiating our sexual desires with porn while we focus on other things... rather than pursuing quick flings, (and the associated bar/Uber tab).

Concerned Elder: You're less desperate than we were hahah

Maybe. Perhaps when we do hook up, and everything is 'working out quite well' we are sticking with that person. Because we are all well aware of the competition out there. So, we are sticking with a good thing when we find it... and for longer.

How this whole instant-porn thing will pan out is still to be determined. It's only been available on our phones for 10-15 years now. Will Millennials and Gen Z, who have used porn consistently since they were young, be able to stop when they get married? Are they obligated to stop? Is watching porn considered cheating? (Millennial women are very, very divided on this. Personally, I don't think it is)

The great porn experiment is ongoing.

Perhaps Millennial sexuality will be divided into two halves: the emotional connections with our real life partners, and the explorations we make on the side using sex toys (a 15 *billion* dollar industry!) and pornography. And pretty soon -- Virtual Reality pornography. Yes, I've tried it. Yes, it's scary.

And as to what this is going to do to marriage is anyone's guess.

Concerned Elder: Dear Lord...

THE INTERNET AND MILLENNIAL SEXUALITY

Concerned Elder: So, what's with all of this gender blending stuff? Pick a team!

Why *do* we see such a high percentage of people who claim to be gender neutral, or non-gendered, or bi-gender, pan-gender, gender-fluid all of sudden? It's because Millennials, and now IGen feel empowered by seeing others who are expressing themselves in their most authentic way. The online LGBTQ community is very strong and vocal.

Millennials don't like having to make a binary decision about anything else in our lives, and gender preference isn't any different. This is why, according to a Fusion Poll of over 1000 Millennials -- 50% of us believe gender is spectrum and not binary, with another 4% being unsure.

This trend is only increasing. In a recent study by the J. Walter Thompson Innovation Group -- only 48% of I-gen (who are currently 13-20 years old) identified as **exclusively heterosexual.** Trend alert: This is going to have huge effects on entertainment and fashion. I think Millennials - and *definitely* the children of Millennials are going to completely redesign sexuality. But delving into this is above of my pay grade.

All I know is the internet has allowed people who were previously marginalized for their alternative sexuality to find their peers.

Many popular YouTuber's and influencers are gay. Most of them have very candid conversations about their sexuality with their fan base, speaking directly into the camera. They reach millions of young people and empower them to embrace their sexuality, whatever it may be. Universities are already adjusting to this new empowerment with gender-neutral bathrooms, etc.

Concerned Elder: So, what you're telling me is the internet is a morass, a giant soup of sex, and dialogue about sexuality, readily available to anyone at any time, and this is encouraging people to open up their definitions of sexuality?

Yes. Click around any porn site for thirty minutes and your definition of human sexuality will be expanded along the way.

But more than that, way we intake this information means the average young person isn't interpreting these porn videos through the lens of religious, or cultural notions of 'virtue', 'righteousness', 'innocence', etc. It all just *is*. It's so clear that sexuality comes in a jillion different flavors. Sorry, Concerned Elder, you're being a little judgmental in my opinion.

THE CORAL REEF: AN ANALOGY FOR MILLENNIALS

Imagine snorkeling off the coast Australia. You look down and see a vast landscape of biodiversity. Corals of every color and shape and form. Some have valves that open and close, some have stalks that sway with the current.

When you're nose deep and the diversity of life is all around you, breathing, and swirling -- the primary emotion is not judgment. It's more intrigue, and curiosity than anything else. You don't hate a piece of coral because it's yellow and spiky, do you?

How silly is it to judge a coral reef for simply being itself? I'm not going to judge it for being colorful, rough, or asymmetrical, flexible, stiff, etc etc. I'm not going to judge the coral reef for wanting to kiss a man over a woman. (oops)

Who am I to judge?

To me, humans do what humans do. We're boundary pushers in every direction. We're constantly trying to express our truest self via our clothes, our language, and our methods of intimacy. So to limit our boundaries in any way is fundamentally against our social nature, as beings that strive to relate to each other on as many levels as possible. Why draw extreme dividing lines between masculinity and femininity? Aren't we all, a mix of both energies? Why put a damper on that process in the sexual realm?

Why limit the experience anyone can have with each other as long as all parties are consenting?

TREND ALERT: ARE YOU PICKING UP A THEME?

Everything, from sexuality to technology to religion is going horizontal. Its opening up, the walls are tumbling down. Everything is becoming less black and white. More connected. More options are available. More parts of more stuff are fitting into more things. How many ways can I say it? This is the new era we are stepping into: **full organic cohesion of pretty much everything.** The floodgates have been opened! The barriers are coming down; the judgment level is coming down.

The trend line is clearly heading toward a laissez-faire culture because the internet has shown us that everything about humans falls on a spectrum of diversity.

Admittedly, this exposure has bred insecurities; because we are comparing ourselves to the best, the brightest, the longest, and cutest that the world has to offer. But it's a relatively small price to pay for being in a more connected society that is in the process of filtering, and exposing our best ideas for all to see.

'Ignorance is bliss' no longer exists. But ignorance can also cause racism, sexism, ritual cannibalism, and all the other horrible-isms.

Concerned Elder: We had all the technology we needed in 1998. Jurassic Park was amazing. We landed on the moon. We could make airline reservations online… we should have stopped there!

No! That's the meta-message of this entire book. Humans are evolving. To reign in our technology, which shapes our world view, which shapes our direction, would be to go against the very idea of humanity: which is to expand in all directions, limitlessly. It's what we have always done. We build new tools to adapt to new challenges. Like organizing seven billion people in an efficient way. The process isn't going to be perfectly smooth. There will be pitfalls, but we can't stop now.

Look what it's already done!

Information has been democratized. With all its imperfections, and pitfalls, the internet is driving behavioral change like nothing in history has before. It's causing people around the word to audit themselves, their beliefs, and their behaviors.

It feels chaotic, and there are still bastions of dissent and backlash about this and that. But we're growing a unified core of young people who are remarkably similar in their core ethic. It's the worldview of laissez faire to the utmost. It's a worldview of constant connection, emotional openness, and acceptance of diversity.

Which we will be needing *a lot of* as we step into the future of virtual reality, photo realistic altered reality experiences, widespread psychedelic usage, multicultural families, automation, intelligent AI, peer to peer finance, computer systems in our bodies and so on.

e.

Chapter 5:
THE MILLENNIAL MIND: SOCIAL MEDIA

Concerned Elder: Don't even get me started on social med---

Please, allow me. (*Inhale*)

Social media is *the* worst thing on planet Earth. It bombards us with a highlight reel of other people's lives, making us neurotic and insecure about our own jobs, friends, wealth, and/or abdominals. It makes us second-guess every life decision for fear that a smarter, better, or more fun option is available. It creates a never-ending desire to be the center of attention, teaching us to define our own self-worth with the number of likes we receive. Constantly updating, highly addictive, and observing us at all times, our viewing habits are analyzed by the finest machine learning algorithms on the planet: studying our psychology so it can figure out how to keep us fixated longer, so it can flash *just one more* ad to us before our eyes glaze over, our tongue falls out, and our brain gives way having been fragmented in too many directions. *Wheeeew!*

Do I actually think this? No. Are there elements of truth to this? Yes. Social media is definitely powerful. But the value it has in our life is entirely up to the user. I, for one, love it. Here's what some other Millennials have to say:

Peter, 27, Australian: "I'm addicted to it, but I hate it. I think it's made us more narcissistic."

Alice, 23, UK: "I think the value of it depends entirely on how it's used. The problems arise when it becomes a literal obsession to share your life and hampers your ability to live in the moment. Or when *you* become so obsessed with other people you stop reflecting on yourself."

Jane, 24: "I'm completely addicted to it. I love it and it inspires me, informs me, and makes me laugh daily."

Christoph 24: "It makes us aware of lots of sh*t, but we are aware of so much stuff, it can be overwhelming and hard to decide what to focus on. Because it feels like there's so much to learn. Also, things seem bleak in terms of the confirmation bias of certain groups."

Emily: "Depends on how you use it. There's garbage and there's gems you'd never find any other way...That's not a very satisfying answer though."

Steve 23: "I think it's almost a total waste of time. I try to completely avoid it. Except I do have a soft spot for the inside jokes that develop on Reddit boards."

SOCIAL MEDIA LETS US CURATE THE INTERNET

Concerned Elders like to point to the Kardashians when they talk about how pointless social media is, but there really is a lot more to it than that. And that's what I'm going to break down. Again, for my younger readers, feel free to skim the next few sections. Because a lot of this is painfully obvious to us.

So, if the internet is the sum total of human activity in terms of articles, videos, images and raw information, then social media is - at its best - a way to curate that knowledge and share it with each other. Notice, I said 'at it's best'. Because it can be a very mixed bag. If you're not careful, sandwiches, selfies, and kitten pictures will dominate your Facebook, Snapchat, and Instagram feeds. But if a person carefully curates who they follow, social media can radically enhance your information sphere. Which is mostly a good thing--except when it distracts us.

. **It's the modern distribution system of cultural ideas.** It connects people with similar tastes, interests, skills, and worldviews in a more *specific* way than ever before. Whether it's a terrific business advice, make-up tutorials, beard growing tips, food trend, life-lesson, or booty pic -- Millennials are sharing gems with each other at a feverish pace.

All of these things spread virally and organically. Viruses in our bodies are bad. But viral information, spread through social media is amazing! (As long as it's not cyber bullying)

What happens is the best stuff rises to the top. And what's great is that anyone in the entire world can contribute! If you put out good content, you will get followers! The best fashion ideas, the best art, the funniest animal memes, the healthiest vegan recipes, etc, etc. Any topic or idea can instantly collect people to it. The best curators win. It's direct publication and instant consumption. **Within my field, I have a rolodex of 50 Instagram accounts that I turn to. They are a form of 'grounding' for me, when I'm either curious, or uninspired.**

There are Instagram pages that are about traveling the world for cheap, starting online businesses, artisanal recipes, homemade candy, DIY, and a lot of other extremely specific niches, which I'm always shocked when I see they have 50,000 followers or more. Like breeding long haired rabbits.

The people who curate these Instagram feeds often live a lifestyle around what they post. So they become authentic leaders in whatever niche they're in. This a profound way to organize and introduce new ideas to culture. It's like watching a certain TV channel and being able to directly interact with the creator of the channel, and talk with the viewers.

And so the channels build a community around them. There are Instagram feeds that are full-on lifestyle hubs. People like Daniel DiPiazza founder of 'Rich20Something' has created what he calls his 'tribe'; basically 230,000 people who are into in his particular mixture of online entrepreneurship, self-improvement, and New Age spirituality. You then join his e-mail list where Daniel writes and curates even more stuff for his followers. I enjoy his work.

Other people might follow fashion guru's like Ingrid Nielson who has 1.7 million followers:

ingridnilsen Follow

88,931 likes   42w

ingridnilsen Last night's vibes celebrating 25 years with one of my all-time faves, @freshbeauty! Loving every minute of this beautiful Parisian experience. Thank you 💜 #fresh25

view all 502 comments

slaysia_ Doctor who companion am I right @jather1ne

sydneyfrenchie @ingridnilsen where'd you get those shoes girl?

wearethe.lgbtq @slaysia_ OMG UR RIGHT

marissarocksss @sshane77

alice.v.izaguirre I need to know where these shoes are from! I love them 💜 @ingridnilsen

johnlovin12 Omg u look like Dillon Harper!!

cecibr96 @carmendg96 cdo t crezca dejatlo asi😂 es mi sueño asiq pa ti

carmendg96 Lo tengo parecido ahora

Add a comment...

These people are 'influencers', or 'thought leaders'; authorities on a given subject.

Of course, mixed in with this stuff, you have your silly friends who post things like:

"HOLY $HIT GUYS I JUST ATE THE MOST AMAZING SUSHI BURRITO BURGER IN SANTA MONICA! #AMAZING #SOFULL

This gets obnoxious. Unless it was like *really* good, then please tag its location for me thnxx ☺

It's really easy to discover new things that can radically enhance your life that you wouldn't have found any other way. The workout regimen that I follow was invented by a guy my age, who I found on Instagram (@Kinobody fitness). Professionally, I have networked with many of my favorite artists in other states because of how often I comment on their work. (Prediction: the Instagram direct message or 'DM' will become the new email location. Calling it now.)

My two biggest lifestyle influencers are probably @Tai Lopez and @Gary Vaynerchuk; both entrepreneurs. Every single day I learn five or six new things about life and business from their posts. Often I write them down in my notebook (or phone, let's be honest...)

These 'influencers' could really just be called my remote mentors. They tell me what to read, how to balance work and life, new business trends, etc. And because I see the fruits of their success everyday, I'm motivated to put in the work or study.

Tai Lopez credits his business success on having read a book a day for over a decade. He gets messages from inner city kids holding stacks of books, telling him they have started reading because of him. Tai has become a social media phenomenon with his message based on the importance of constant learning to be successful.

Tech Investor and CEO Gary Vaynerchuk is a similar educational influencer. He actually has a cameraman follow him around every single day as he runs his nine-figure advertising agency, VaynerMedia in New York. Over the two years of daily vlogging, he has purchased companies, launched new departments, launched a full-fledged sports agency, and even created a holding company called VanyerX. Now that's some wholesome reality TV… He gives epic motivational speeches as well, and is a 4x best selling author. With over three million followers he is easily one of the most influential- of influencers. As in, he actually influences the way people *lead their lives*, not the color of their make up. The guy can't hardly walk around in New York without someone saying how he changed their lives… wow.

These guys are pioneering the growing 'edu-tainment' space. They understand education should be about leading with the excitement of the topic. This is the educational model of the future. Seeing others do it; seeing the rewards of their passion in the topic, and following along with them each day.

People who criticize influencers for monetizing their influence are dead wrong. Tai sells courses. Gary gives speeches and sells books. Great. They'll see the Lambos' and the Beverly Hills mansion in Tai's videos and criticize him for spreading materialism. But he's genuinely sharing insanely good life advice. And when he does offer formal courses you know it's not BS.

My friends and I are constantly sharing these types of posts with each other. This is the purest joy one can have on social media. Being able to virtually wave your arms in the air and yell "Hey, I've found something cool!" Isn't that a beautiful thing?

MANY OF US HAVE AN INTIMATE BOND WITH OUR INFLUENCERS

Our influencers usually have some aspect of life that we want or admire. And believe me, we can get really, *really* attached these people. Because we digitally hang out with them every day.

Concerned Elder: Sounds like these influencers are like our old movie stars –

The difference is that we spend so much intimate time with these people, they can start to feel like your best friends... and I say that with complete sincerity. My influencers have been a nice supplement to my art school education, which has been a lot of sitting in my room working alone.

Prior to really embracing social media, I didn't have clear role models. I was so trapped in my desire to build my skills that I wasn't thinking of the bigger picture. What did I *really* care about besides art? What did I want my life to *feel* like on a daily basis?

My influencers made me think more holistically. They have given me pieces to the puzzle of life that I wasn't getting from anywhere else because I had my head down working ten hours a day. It was the perfect counter balance for me.

You'll notice Millennials love talking about what activities we would do even if no one paid us. And this is because we've had so much exposure to people who have built really cool lives doing what they love. We know it's possible. It's why many of us are more focused on building healthy lifestyles than achieving wealth or job status. We're not as big on possessions as previous generations. The high cost of living in big cities has made many of us dream of simply having a decent place to live.

Most of us have grown up around at least a few adults who hate their job and have seen how it affects their lives. We've felt that ickyness, so maybe we have become obsessed with avoiding that.

Whether it's a home-chef guru who boxes her meals and delivers them with her dogs in tow, or an artist who sells customized items on their Etsy Store, or a blogger who gets to travel for a living, we get these windows into people's who have 'integrated their career and their life', which is really what most Millennials strive for,

Having access to people like this can be highly motivating, but it has its drawbacks. It's easy to forget the work it took to get to there. We see the end product, the glamorous Instagram posts, but we don't see the years where they had their head down, reading, studying, and working on their career.

You do see disheartened comments. The art community is the hardest on themselves. Nicholas 'Sparth' Bouvier will be pumping out masterpiece after masterpiece each day. People will comment, "I'll never be this good!" or "I wish I had your gift," forgetting the twenty years he's worked at it.

Social media can definitely fuel certain people's insecurities because it's almost a real-time comparison, between what *you're* doing, and what *they're* doing. Which of course can lead to second-guessing your own talent and choices in life.

I might be sitting at home writing my book, only to see 20 year-old rapper, Lil Yachty, sitting in his purple Bentley with four beautiful women. And he's talking to *me*, and ten thousand other people... *live.*

How do you handle situations like this? Does it motivate you or does it discourage you? Or could you care less what Lil' Yachty is doing? The answer is different for each person. As Bailey Parnell aptly points out in her TED Talk, "When you talk about the dark side of social media, you're really talking about the dark side of people."

INFLUENCERS AND ADVERTISING

The influencer phenomenon is a marketer's wet dream and nightmare at the same time. It's easy to know where people's eyeballs are by looking at follower counts. So, advertising your product nowadays is as simple as paying the right influencer to use it. This is how Tom Bilyeu grew Quest Nutrition into a *billion dollar* company in about seven years. By organically interlocking his product with influencers who reached his target audience. But it's complicated because many influencers are marketing their *own* products now.

As the barriers to entry in many industries continue to come down, the competition over the best, healthiest, tastiest, fastest, most organic, most artisanal stuff has intensified dramatically. Say, you're a makeup brand that specializes in all natural pigments in certain specialty colors. There's probably an influencer who would love your product and would show it off perfectly to their million-plus followers. But when these influencers get big enough -- they might just start their own brand of make-up. Because *they* are the face that people recognize. This is how Kylie Jenner will soon be richer than all her sisters combined. And she did it in about 2 years.

Kylie aside, in the long run this is great for the consumer because products are evolving faster and getting more specific to our needs. Bad products are weeded out by influencers who review them, or who refuse to advertise the ones they don't like. Not in all cases, *yet*, but that's the trend. As GaryVee puts it, "We are on the verge of humanizing business."

SOCIAL MEDIA AND SELF ESTEEM ISSUES

Concerned Elder (Dad): But isn't this destroying the American work ethic? Not everyone can be a rapper, play videogames for a living, be a YouTuber, be good-looking or be entrepreneurs. We need people to do ordinary jobs; electricians, plumbers, etc…

I do think social media stars makes *some* people feel bad about living a regular life. But not everyone wants to conquer the world, be the best, the brightest, the richest. And for these people, their influencers will be of an entirely different sort. Shane Dawson is a perfect example. He's a top YouTuber who can't decide if he's gay, has major body issues, loves exploring the weirdest parts of the internet, and has a great sense of humor about it all.

My girlfriend's Lil'-Yachty-in-a-Bentley moment might come in the form of her favorite YouTuber pulling off some hilarious prank. Or her favorite concept artist successfully crowd funding their art book. These things might make her feel jealous, but they also inspire her. The two are almost always linked.

In fairness, we *are* over exposed to people "on the extreme ends of the bell curve", as author Mark Manson puts it in his best-selling book *'The Subtle Art of Not Giving A F*ck'*. Sometimes, we forget that being totally average is in fact quite normal. Yes, this is a danger of social media - fixating on what you're not...

This is why sociologists have blamed social media for making teens desperate to be the center of attention.

And it's definitely true for some of us. We all know people who define their self-esteem by how many followers they have. People who take 300 selfies to find just the right one. Or teens who take 'bad' photos down if they don't get enough likes within ten minutes.

But I think for most of us, social media is more meaningful then that. Yes, I said *meaningful.* It's about interacting with people of similar interests. It's about exploring what's happening 'out there'. I think, when we see something inspiring, it causes most of us to look at ourselves in a deeper way.

That's what happened to me. Before I found my big influencers, I was in a rut. I was filling that void by pouring myself into studying, but without a clear direction. My inspiration was running low, so my art sucked, and I was pretty unhappy. In other words, I was burning out before my career even began.

The ecosystem of different opportunities, jobs, sales channels, etc., that I learned about on social media, made me realize that I needed to take some time away from art college and completely re-analyze everything about myself. Temporary anger, and a bit of jealousy, were all part of that process. In fact, the impetus for this book came out of that period of my life.

Let's just get down to brass tacks: seeing people who are flaunting their triumphs can be motivation or it can ruin you. But I'd reckon for every one person that is left dismayed, there are five more that are left inspired.

Not enough people talk about the creativity boost that social media can give you.

What if I combined GaryVee's drive and optimism, with Tai Lopez's improvement methodology, with Joe Rogan's open mindedness, and Sparth's artistic techniques? All in service of expanding the human 'thought potential'? (A term I got from Terrence McKenna, whom I learned about from Duncan Trussel's podcast.)

That might be on the outer edge of my potential. But it took six or seven influencers to get me to that grand vision that I can be excited about. I'm a grand vision type of guy. I didn't even know that was thing till Tai told me it was.

By the way, the names I underlined could be many different people. Anyone. My point is, seeing others achieve success makes me want to chase my own form of success.

Dad: HOW ABOUT GETTING A NORMAL, GOOD OLD-FASHIONED JOB?! IN AN OFFICE! WITH A PAYCHECK!

I'm writing this book, dad! *Then,* I'm getting a job... (jeez)

JUMPING BETWEEN COMMUNITIES

There are different layers within social media and the internet. And this is how the **'meta-verse'** is formed. It's the combination of multiple communities, sharing and curating certain kinds of content.

If you're a Millennial this is painfully obvious, but I gotta' make sure I cover all the bases for my old-timer readers.

So, there are different tiers of political correctness and then, within each tier, you have influencers, sharers, curators, etc. For instance, someone might share something inappropriate on a Reddit or Tumblr board that they wouldn't dream of posting on Facebook or LinkedIn because those platforms are linked to their actual identity. Naturally, users of Reddit and picture meme websites are known to host some of the most hilarious (and sometimes most offensive) kinds of content. Inside jokes and memes tend to stack onto each other deep in the underbelly of Reddit, often with strange results...

Once we discover content we like, we interact within that community. You read the posts, then, you read comments on what *other* people think of each post. Of course there's always the stupid comments from trolls, but often you can find thoughtful conversations happening. Millennials love reading comments about stuff. We love the **meta-analysis**.

The large majority of Millennials are navigating in multiple social communities each day, often minute to minute.

Concerned Elder: It sounds exhausting, frankly...

We jump around a lot, and we know what to expect on each platform. My social media 'stack' consists of:
- digital artists
- figure drawing experts
- rappers
- business influencers
- science and cosmos stuff
- wild life photography
- humanitarian content

- and horribly absurd internet content like this:

My girlfriend's stack would be:

- Disney fan made content

- Animation Artists

- Cosplay Content (dressing up as fantasy characters)

- make up tutorials

- cat pictures

- cat memes

- fashion influencers

- social justice Tumblr posts (people sharing sad stories)
- weird offensive memes

You can tell a lot about a person by who and what constitutes their Instagram/ Tumblr feeds. Notice, we both like weird internet content. A big percentage of Millennials have a taste for absurdity; it's an acquired taste from years of sharing weird stuff as middle-school kids.

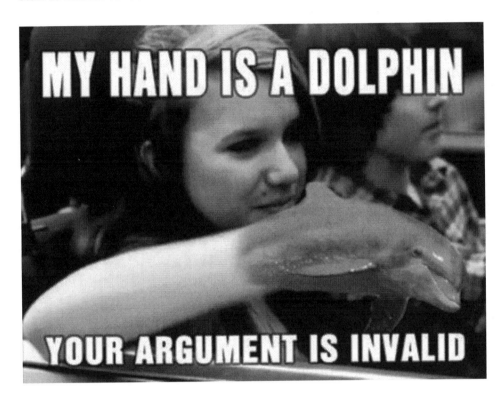

Concerned Elder: I don't get it….

Exactly.

CULTURE MINING

This mix of ideas was hard to achieve in the past. Everyone was more hermetically sealed from each other either socially or geographically…

But *if* we curate our social media, podcasts, and the greater collection of online resources it's now possible to 'mine' (a videogame term) any and all communities for the wisdom that they curate best. The technical term is finding **'information funnels'**.

The GaryVee community is all about hustle and self awareness.

The Tai Lopez community is all about self improvement strategies.

My yoga influencers are always talking about hip flexor activation after sitting for 6 hours.

My fitness influencers introduced me to intermittent fasting.

My art influencers are all about_____

My tech influencers foresee _____ on the horizon.

My_____ influencer focuses on_____.

My_____ influencer tells me_____.

My_____ influencer showed me that_____.

All of these things form a collage of… of… influences! That radically shape your life and expand your info-sphere.

These posts eventually become different mindsets that are a part of you. Or, better yet, they give you 'permission' to accept aspects of yourself as *actually* viable. A lesson I learned from Joe Rogan was that being completely childish, ridiculous, and whip smart is totally possible at the ripe age of 49. He showed me a type of person I didn't know existed, simply by being himself.

The diversity of communities on social media shows a person that they don't have to stick to the set of ideas they grew up with. It can be weird how you hear just the thing you need at the right time. Serendipity. Like when I got super into listening to UFC fighters talk about their training regimes. It made me radically change my own approach to learning design.

But searching for these realizations, having them, and adjusting, can be stressful and painful, and everyone handles this process differently.

BRANDING YOURSELF VS. BEING YOURSELF

Meta-analysis: Staying cognizant of the perspective, or the lens that a post is coming from is an essential skill when you're in-taking so much information from so many different sources each day.

With one half-glance, I could tell you what the 'slant' will be of each of these tiles on Instagram. And probably what type of person posted it.

There's a lot to gain by comparing what one community prioritizes vs. another. What is considered trivial in one community, might be heavily valued in another.

For instance, in the art community and the rap community, being spontaneous, wild, and flashy is highly valued. But strategy is valued the most in business circles. Yet these two communities are a mere swipe away from each other and I relate to both.

In the NBA community, flashiness is valued but so is work ethic and professionalism. It's almost like the NBA community is a mixture of artistic and business sensibilities.

This goes back to my point about building emotional intelligence. I'm always asking, 'What's the background of the poster?' We are constantly juxtaposing these 'meta' viewpoints or else we wouldn't be able to make sense of it all.

And then many of us start playing a version of this game in our head:

"What would a business person say about *my* approach to my life? Versus, what would the most free-spirited artsiest person I know of say about my life? I might not be business oriented enough nor artsy enough for either. Is that a bad thing? Am I a healthy blend? Or am I hedging my bets? AHHHHH!"

And it can lead to a lot of second guessing yourself. I think a lot of us struggle with **branding ourselves vs. being ourselves.** What if you don't think your true self is very attractive to community x? Is it wrong to adapt your public persona? Or are you potentially giving up your special sauce that could have been your like-able advantage? Millennials do a lot of this self-analysis. (This is why bosses that embrace our quirkiness are very much appreciated Tip: share weird memes with your younger employees, they'll love you for it.)

Concerned Elder: We didn't have so many influences. We just had to jump in and figure it out!

I'm actually sort of jealous of your simpler times. We can spend days searching for the best ways to do something. But it can easily lead to 'planning paralysis'; over-thinking things, as opposed to trusting your intuitive side.

A TYPICAL TWO MINUTES ON SOCIAL MEDIA

Here is a typical two minutes on my Instagram.

Followed by :

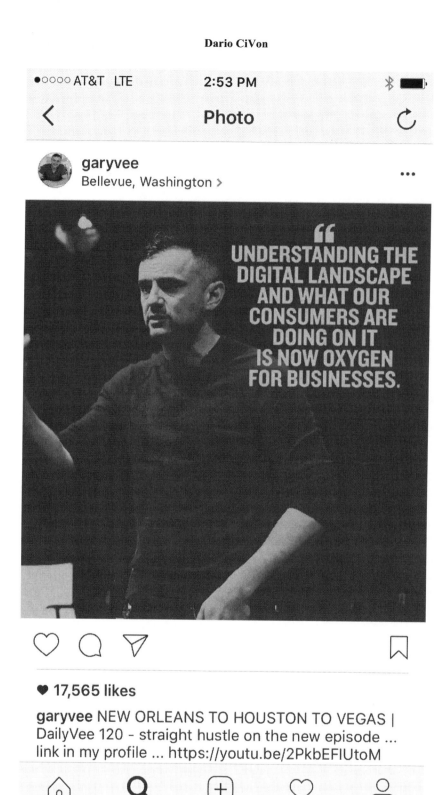

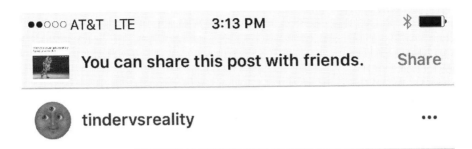

●●ooo AT&T LTE   3:13 PM   ⁜ ▬

You can share this post with friends.   Share

tindervsreality   •••

When your squad gets absolutely fucked up at the club

♡ ◯ ▽   ⊓

▶ 201,294 views

tindervsreality Tag yo squalla @tindervsreality

View all 2,282 comments

Whah?

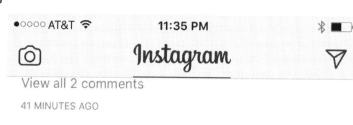

View all 2 comments

41 MINUTES AGO

metromarketermag

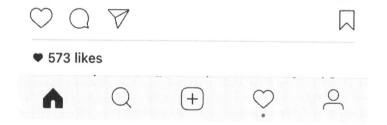

**8 Rules
2 Kick Ass In Life**

1. See failure as a beginning, not an end.
2. If you don't go after it, you won't have it.
3. Always do more than is expected of you.
4. Assume nothing and question everything.
5. Make peace with the past or you'll pay for it.
6. Stop thinking so much and start acting.
7. Never compare yourself to others.
8. Teach others what you know.

♥ 573 likes

Followed by:

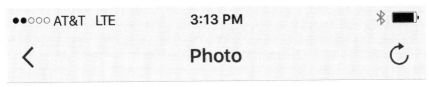

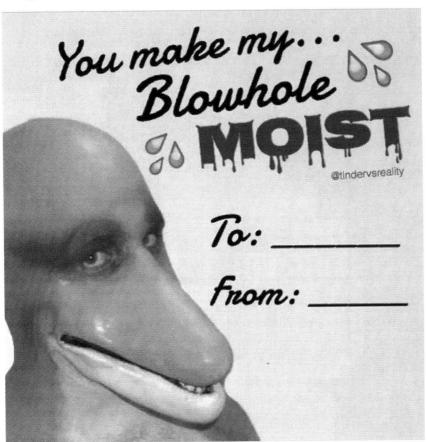

6,370 likes

tindervsreality Tag someone who makes your blowhole moist 💦💦💦💦💦 part 1 of my beautiful E-Card series

And then:

●○○○○ AT&T LTE   3:43 PM   ＊ ▬

<   Photo   ↻

tailopez
Oslo, Norway >   •••

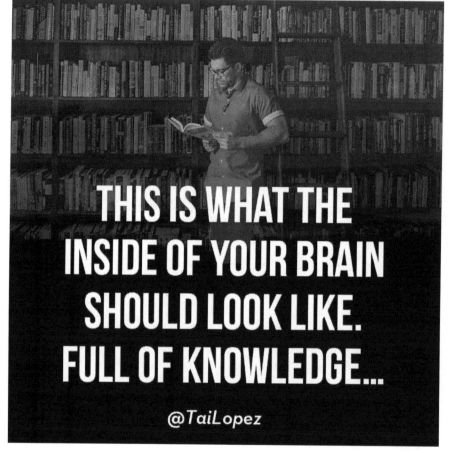

THIS IS WHAT THE
INSIDE OF YOUR BRAIN
SHOULD LOOK LIKE.
FULL OF KNOWLEDGE...

@TaiLopez

♡   ◯   ◁   ⊓

♥ 28,609 likes

tailopez I mean it as a metaphor, obviously you don't
want me reading a book inside your head haha😳...
#readersareleaders

⌂   Q   ⊕   ♡   ◯

Concerned Elder: I'm so confused...

Of course you are. Going back to my general thesis on Millennials: **we are not closed off from much.** The next swipe could be *anything*. Our lives are filled with strange imagery, advice, other people's adventures, kittens, videogames, memes, and 'life hacks'. **Our information diet is diverse, but ultimately the dialogues we will have with each other will be diverse.**

MANY INFLUENCERS ARE CENTERED AROUND PURE FUN

Thus far, I've focused on social media for self-improvement. But the reality is that many of the biggest influencers are simply people who are fun to virtually hang out with. They are regular, relatable people that talk in front of a camera. This is the heart of the current "Lets Play" phenomenon on YouTube and TwitchTV right now. Channels like Game Grumps, Markiplier, PewDiePie, KSI and dozens of others, feature someone simply recording themselves playing videogames and just plain having a good old' time. It's like comfort food. They just make you feel good.

There's a 'Let's Play' star for every personality type at this point. If you prefer good looks and a sexy deep voice, then Markiplier is your man. If you prefer totally berserk, curse filled rampages than DashieGames is your guy. Oddly, my girlfriend is addicted to the latter.

Me: Why do you like watching Dashie scream and curse like a madman?

Jane: Even though he screams and shouts, I somehow can relate in a weird way! He sort of embodies the little angry child in all of us. He's not even that good at games and neither am I. I use him as a way to vent my own anger lol.

There you go.

YouTube, and social media is allowing new types of social 'celebrities' to be made, not hulking athletes or larger than life actors and singers. These internet stars are in essence, millions of people's good friends. And they get paid *very* handsomely. I think this is fantastic (and another source of instant emotional comfort for Millennials and Gen Z.)

PewDiePie, is one of the most famous YouTubers. He makes over ten million dollars a year playing videogames, watching silly videos, and messing around for his 50 million subscribers. He puts out an episode everyday, which means, on occasion, he's gotten into trouble with some misguided ideas for his shows.

But the connection these YouTube stars have with their fans is intense. They get people who write to them about how their shows got them through serious depression or illness. And of course, they make new videos reading these fan notes to their fans (usually while crying).

The rise of the 'average joe' influencers like Shane Dawson, Tyler Oakley, Rhett James, or Link Neal have providing needed comfort to millions and millions of people. That's social media at its best.

Concerned Elder: Do these 'regular joe's' have other talents besides playing video games and talking on camera?

Their talent is being likeable and relatable. Most of the time they are just chatting into the camera about everyday stuff. Sometimes they do weird 'challenges' they invent. Like Jenna Marbles putting on 50 layers of make-up; or making Frankenstein food (combining strange foods like spaghetti sauce and chocolate cake). Sometimes, YouTubers have their fans send them the weirdest 'cringe' videos they can find. They film 'try not to laugh' challenges. My girlfriend and I love watching these together.

Sometimes they talk about emotional problems or just vent about a topic. It's just super friendly content, with a heavy self-awareness factor. (Self-awareness is **the key** to connecting with Millennials).

When college kids begrudgingly give up videogames, they often switch to these 'Let's Play's of other people playing. That's what I've done. It's like watching a movie with funny friends. And of course, there is the meta component, when we read the comments to see if other people laugh at the same parts that we did.

Watching someone play a game for others to comment on -- and then have them read the comments back to the viewers in real time -- is confusing to write, but actually really fun. It's content in multiple dimensions.

It can get *even more meta* though. One of my teachers said that his 13 year-old daughter will often:
- play a game
- while Skyping with multiple friends
- while they all watch the same 'lets play' video of their favorite YouTube gamer who's playing and commenting in real time.
- while texting other friends
- while they *all* play that *same game* together online

That's five tiers of meta thinking going on... iGen is on another level. In fact multiple Millennials with siblings have independently said to me 'If they think *we're* weird, just wait for iGen. They're a whole different breed!". You've been warned.

Concerned Elder: The human race is doomed...

No! It's the opposite! The more real time connectivity, the better. *'The more meta the betta'* in my opinion, because they're going to bring that 'multi-tiered' mindset to everything they do in life.

Here is a picture meme that sums up this 'meta' idea perfectly.

Concerned Elder (my friend's Mom): I still don't get it...

You just can't handle the *meta-ness*.

MILLENNIALS DON'T WATCH REGULAR TV

YouTube videos and videogames are a huge reason that Millennials watch considerably less regular television. It's because online content can be perfectly customized to our exact emotional needs of the moment. **It's more self aware than film, more personalized, and we crave that.** Often the fans shape the content. Inside jokes get built up within communities over time, and it's addicting to us.

Here are the top thirteen most popular types of videos on YouTube (The order may change by the time of publication.)

1. Product Reviews
2. Tutorials
3. Vlogs (video-blogging. Some vloggers like Charles Trippy, post every day)
4. Gaming/Lets Play'
5. Comedy Skits (ex. Miranda Sings)
6. Haul Videos (go shopping and show us what you bought!)
7. Trending Memes ('Putting Makeup on my Boyfriend' or 'Eating Hot Peppers Challenge'
8. Favorites/Best Of (influencer recommending their favorite things)
9. Educational Videos (TED Talks etc.)
10. Unboxing Videos (watch as I open this brand new--fill in the blank---and react to it)
11. Q&A Videos (people answering fan questions)
12. Collection Videos (collections of stuffs)
13. Prank Videos (some of these online pranksters have made millions)

Clearly we *really* like watching other people react to things. So, even though our face is buried in our cellphone in the waiting room at the dentist's office... **Millennials are insanely social.**

A typical hour on YouTube is like walking from one friend's house to another, then another. It's very comforting and nonthreatening... even if they are playing cartoonishly violent videogames sometimes. That's the Millennial dichotomy for ya...

Concerned Elder (my friend's Dad): It sounds unbelievably f***ing stupid...

Hahaha. Wow.

SOCIAL MEDIA / INTERNET SPEAK

The rise of social media and online video content has meant that many odd internet phrases are now entering into everyday speech. Phrases like:

"That hit me right in the childhood" (Reminds me of my childhood)

"Goalz" or *"This is goals."* Or "GOALZ AS FU*K". (Typically written under a picture. Meaning, omg this is a goal of mine.)

"This kitten video gives me the feelz" (This touches me emotionally, or pulls at my heart strings)

"I can't even…" (Meaning: I can't look at this. I can't take it.)

'THE STRUGGLE IS REAL" ('Struggle' is used a lot nowadays)

"They got flamed" (Someone got chewed up in the comments section)

" A flame war" (Two people, or factions, duking it out online)

"Are we getting trolled?" (Is someone intentionally writing stupid stuff just to invoke a reaction?)

WIN (Anything that yields progress)

Other phrases include:

'Yes that's a thing' (Meaning, it exists) Ex: *"Have you heard of the flying lawn mower"? "Yes that's a thing".* (Side note: look up the flying lawn mower video. It's hilarious.)

'What is my life?' (What has my life come to?)

If someone is having trouble doing just about anything, you might hear *'you're doing it wrong'*. Ex:
> *"you're pizza-ing wrong'*
> *'you're homeworking wrong'*
> *'you're grammar'ing wrong'*

Another internet phrase is *'in RL'*. Meaning in 'real life'. If something you're saying sounds too crazy, someone might just say *'wait, in RL?'* to confirm you're not talking about something on the internet, (Because we all know it *exists* on the internet. Duh.)

WARNING:
> If you're over fifty, use these at your own risk. (These phrases are still used self-consciously even by us.)
> And, of course there's the good old trusty image memes, which can't be beaten for their wit and sarcasm and hard to explain in words-ness. So, I'll just show you some more of them.

(We've all felt like this cat before)

Meme's are a celebration of the world's stereotypes and weirdness.

There's a youthful 'explorative' quality to these things that shows a sarcastic yet insightful view of the world. They represent the snarky side of what is an overall increased level of self awareness about everything in life. They are a fundamental pillar of millennial humor.

(EXPOSURE ALERT: Think about the variety of people and environments you just saw^)

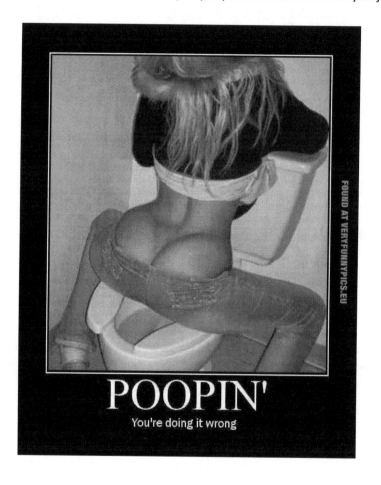

At one time, ten to fifteen years ago, you could only find these images with captions in obscure, lowbrow message boards. Now, memes are found on all layers of the web. They tend to share three common traits.

- they contain a totally random picture + caption
- they are witty
- A majority of people have experienced what the meme is exploring

As I explained in the previous chapter, technically, memes are the smallest unit of any idea. But casually speaking, the term 'meme' refers to: **using random pictures to express something that would be hard to capture in words.**

They are kind of like the inside jokes of the internet culture…. They really are a new form of communication, invented by Millennials. Our iGen little cousins should thank us.

More memes:

Or this guy.

This is a very famous older meme. It's the 'too high guy'. It's a picture of some random college kid. Who knows whether he was actually too high? But he is now the icon for saying stupid stuff while inebriated.

There are thousands of these memes, all of made by random people on various meme-creation websites. You can upload your own pictures and caption them in minutes.

There are memes making fun of every class, creed, race, profession and belief system. I have kept it *very* tame for you because I'm now a published author and have a reputation to protect.

But, if I'm being completely honest, many memes can be racist or play upon stereotypes. On the surface, this isn't good. But on the other hand, the over-the-top nature of them tend to push these things into the realm of satire. Memes can disarm stereotypes with their tasteful-tastelessness...if that makes sense? There are memes about *anything*.

One of my favorite memes is the 'Philoso-raptor'. it's the raptor from Jurassic Park tackling life's hardest questions. It's a satire on man's desire for logic and reason...

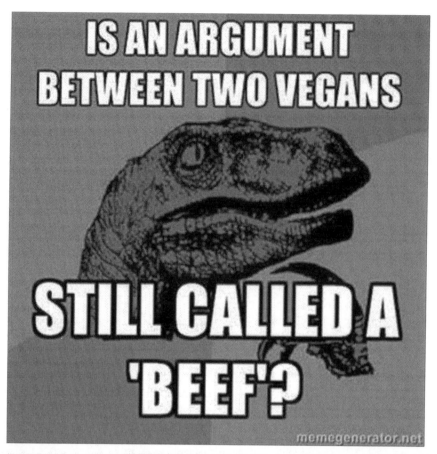

Memes have profoundly influenced almost every millennial's sense of humor.

But sometimes they have an actual utility.

MEMES ARE A DATING TOOL

Memes are used heavily when two people begin dating. They are among the first things people send to each other when they flirt online -- perhaps after the emoji's settle down a bit. They are a good way of gaging the other person's level of sensitivity and sense of humor. If they don't like the same memes as you, you probably aren't a match.

Concerned Elder (my friend's mom): What?? You guys really are aliens!

I knew kids in high school that would rather send you memes than write messages.

If I asked them "how are you" on Facebook, I would get:

If I asked how they like their classes, they would respond:

If they were in a good mood she might send me :

This is the stoned dog meme. An older one.

My girlfriend is obsessed with cuteness, so I can't tell you how many times I've gotten these pictures.

Concerned Elder (friend's mom): This is all so weird...

Critics of memes, and emoji's claim that Millennials aren't learning to express themselves properly. That our ability to communicate verbally is dumbed down. And you know what? I agree.

I've met people that literally need memes to communicate., or are far better at typing then speaking.

RELATING YOURSELF TO WEIRD PICTURES

Simply put, **young people are visually sophisticated** because we have consumed more images than probably all generations combined! Not to mention we spend half our lives looking at screens.

We like it when we see elements of ourselves in animals and other people. I'm not saying older people don't, but they definitely don't tag themselves in weird pictures and say "This is meeee" like Millennials do. Or tag our friends to it.

"This is youuuu."

'The Titanic sank with approximately 3000 pounds of garlic bread on board'

Me:

(Translation: This is joke about how people adore garlic bread... and they'll do anything for it.)

"LITERALLY MY LIFE" – random Instagram user

^This is the praying beaver meme. Very useful.

Whether it's frogs, snakes, jockeys, or weird looking Disney characters - we love when we see a spark of ourselves in random pictures. Why do we do it? It's sort of a new way of satire...sort of?

This behavior is a finer point of being a Millennial/GenZ/iGen but the inclusion of imagery as part of our communication is something that is only going to continue. In fact apple just released Animoji's that change form based on your own facial data.

These visual forms of communication, if done tastefully can be hilarious and a perfectly valid part of discourse. As long we don't abandon vocabulary all together.

MEMES AND MARKETING

Millennials can sense sarcasm from a mile away. We love dry humor like the memes above, but conversely we like it when we can sense 'realness' (another Millennial term). We can sniff out phony advertisements in a snap.

This is why marketing to Millennials has split off in two directions. One direction is utilizing the over-the top-snarky lingo and absurd visuals like the famous 'Pug Monkey Baby' ad, by Mountain Dew, for the 2015 Superbowl. It's odd, it's memorable, and we love that.

We want more of this^

The other direction is towards ultra sincere forms of marketing. Hence, the trend toward very simple packaging and very simple sales pitches.

This is Millennials in a nutshell: **We are either being very sincere and genuine, or exercising our snarky and flamboyant side. We don't hang around in the middle.** Millennials relate the 'hard-sell' to cold corporate boardrooms, not to a genuine desire to add value. We love it when brands donate a portion of their profits to good causes. We want to know that our dollars are going to help people, and not simply enrich the CEO and hurt Gaia. In fact, in the 2016 Millennial Impact Report, Millennials turn to businesses over politics to exercise their desire to help the world. 'Buy one, give one' brands, such as Tom's shoes or Warby Parker, are very popular.

Why are we this way? For one, many of us can't remember a time when our political system worked smoothly, but also because of our exposure to the nasty aspects of manufacturing shared on social media. Hence the rise of Indy, Hipster, DIY, homemade, artisanal, organic, craft, sustainably produced, crowdfunding, crowdsourcing, ultra-customizable, etc. All of these popular millennial cultural pillars are direct rejections of what we perceive as cold, old fashioned, less conscious corporate systems.

WHAT WE NEED MORE YOUNG PEOPLE DOING #2

Millennials really care about doing 'meaningful work'. It's kind of hot button with us. I've come to realize that meaningful work, or spirit work, or whatever you want to call it, means bearing the psychological burden of a particular problem. Like, really feeling it, maybe even crying about it. And then having the fortitude to host the dialogues on social media , *while* implementing some solution. Doing both is the key.

These are what I would call **Stage 2 Influencers**. Not just Influencers who are comforting, funny, and then toss an advertisements at you at the end of their video. We need Influencers who see gaps in society, and are actively filling the hole, while hosting the conversation about it. This is where social media is heading. The gamers and makeup influencers just got there first...

I firmly believe that we are living through **'The Era of Stitching'**. Or the 'Era of Unification.' A movement towards viewing all parts of society as one thing.

Right now, the many different spheres of society have gathered lot of data/knowledge about specific areas. Most of the really valuable work that's left to be done, is in the **connective tissue**. Connecting all of the established pockets, so that they flow together better. For instance, my familiarity with old master paintings is of great use to the videogame industry. But that's a tiny example. What if a musician's understanding of flows and rhythms, could unlock more potential in athletes? We need Stage 2 influencers making these intellectual leaps. There's connective work to be done every direction! People who see holes, talk about it, and bridge those gaps through new types of discussions, and businesses, And so parents, if your child is interested in doing this type of work, let them! But it may take a few years at home...

We could use thousands more of these Stage 2 Influencers. This is the new world. Where the lines of dialogue, commerce, service, influence, need, outrage, desire, reaction, feedback; all of these things become integrated at a higher rate. Because the feedback loops will be super tight between them all, through social media. Basically this is the warming, or the feminizing of society. This is what GaryVee means when he says 'We are about to humanize business'. And this is why he documents his life so religiously. He's teaching the younger generations, as he lives. And he's beloved for it.

Ghandi was once asked to send a message back to his village before stepping on onto a train. And he replied: "My life is my message". Social media allows anyone to have their lives work be their message. Any one can become a mini-Ghandi nowadays, in the area that most inspires them.

I TOLD YOU ABOUT THE GOOD – NOW THE BAD AND UGLY

Ok, now for the bad parts of social media... cuz it's 'A THING'.

Yes, it's true... looking down at our phones prevents us from interacting in RL as much as we would otherwise. I think Millennials don't mind talking; we just aren't big conversation *starters...* the social exchange is in cyberspace.

For all the images we've seen, we've probably spoken fewer words per year than any other generation. Most of us report that we'd rather text than talk over the phone. This is why a lot of mentors are advising Millennials to learn the art of public speaking -- because it's definitely in decline.

Ever hear of Facebook Depression? It's the feeling of dismal underachievement you get after you check social media. This is because people only tend to post their accomplishments, the coolest thing they did this week, their fabulous vacations, gourmet meals, etc. It creates a false impression that everyone but you is kicking-ass at life.

We all know Millennials whose entire life is designed around their social media image. They treat selfies like it's a competitive sport. Every pic they take is run through ten filters to make their skin look angelic. Their desire to *appear* a certain way is obvious. The irony is that they are probably exactly the opposite in real life. They post one crazy party pic after the next, so you'd never guess their biggest fear is being unwanted. Being around these people is obnoxious because they aren't living in the moment. They're constantly on the lookout for the next photo-op. And frankly, they are contributing to collective insecurity. It's friggin' annoying.

Social media *has* put a lot of emphasis on **extrinsic shit**; awards, money, cars, abs, bikini bodies, who you're hanging with, etc. As speaker Steven Furtick put it, "We struggle with insecurity because we compare our behind-the-scenes with everyone else's highlight reel."

COMMUNITY CATHARSIS

Fewer people will write about that two-week long depression they had in mid-February. Though, this is changing. When people *do* let it all hang out on social media, they are often showered with encouragement. So I think it's becoming a 'thing' now, because my friends are getting older, and have real problems now... and ewww.

I've learned quite a lot from Facebook friends sharing their low points. My VR artist friend Emily, writes about her struggles with self-confidence so brilliantly that anyone can gain from her insights. People who have had similar struggles collect in the comment section and it becomes a big group conversation.

I asked her why she does this: "When people are scrolling through their feeds, I think they are craving real, genuine, meaningful social connection. I like to share parts of my life that are authentic, sometimes vulnerable, because it's *actually real...* and I know I'm not the only one going through things. When I organize my thoughts and put them out there, it's no longer just mine. It's something others can own if they identify with it, hopefully they will feel less alone in their journey." I think she's spot on.

Millennials also post about their struggles in finding work. Here is a typical post from Ann: "Going to Walmart to try and get a job. It's been difficult to get out of the parent's basement, because I'm not meeting income requirements for available apartments in the entire city except in questionable locations. But I will be alright! I have some freelance coming, which will help build my resume, but it won't pay for more two weeks ☹"

Ann makes posts like these so often she has actually flipped the Facebook Depression formula on its head. Some people *come away* from Facebook depressed. She goes to Facebook depressed, reads all the supportive comments, and comes away happier This is emotional support done right!

SOCIAL MEDIA, ANXIETY, AND MICHAELANGELO

This isn't a self-help book but here's my advice to other Millennials and Gen X'ers dealing with social media jealousy: unfollow people that *really get under your skin* with their achievements. Everyone has their hot buttons; mine might be pretty women in Bentley's. Yours might be seeing stacks of cash, six pack abs, or videos of amazing concerts that you weren't at. Unfollow it. Get it off your feed. You're not going to suddenly forget about that *thing*, and jealously fixating doesn't get you anywhere.

A study performed by the University of Pittsburg showed that using social media for more than two hours a day led to increased feelings of social isolation. But the study didn't determine causality. In other words, perhaps people who use SM that much might already feel isolated and are trying fill an emotional void. (I suspect this is the case because that's exactly how *I* was using it for an entire year. And yes, I was socially isolated, ironically, while I was attending a college.)

Social media and the greater internet robs many Millennials of just simply feeling good in their own skin. There, I said it.

It's also has made us more stressed, because we access it 24/7 from our phones or laptops. This creates the bad habit of not completely shutting down. We don't detach. **We let unimportant thoughts create fuzz balls in our brain.** This has been shown to increase stress levels and lower sleep quality.

The faster our phones get, the more shit we do on them. We think we're good multitaskers, but studies show that humans aren't good at it. It's wreaking havoc on our internal peace. The reality for most of us is that we resemble jugglers more then we resemble Michelangelo spending three years carving one statue in near silence.

Christoph says it well: "Everything about our phone is about the 'other'. The 'something else', rather than the moment." Our culture puts little importance on how life feels internally. Who cares if you're a balanced, healthy individual? What do you do for a living?! Faster, cheaper, better is the game most people are playing.

Our phones have increased our baseline cortisol levels, one of the main stress hormones that causes inflammation, nervousness, angst, stress, even digestive trouble.

We are all juggling too many damn things. We have too many choices to go eat, things to watch, games to play, people to talk to, shit to learn about, expectations we place on ourselves etc etc.   We aren't relaxing properly; we aren't taking care of our bodies. We have high expectations, for ourselves (fueled by the things we see on social media) and it's 'Go go go!' until we get there. Or were the other type of person, who is so lost in a soup of input they don't know where to start, or what they really care about.

Roughly 70% of Millennials want to be entrepreneurs at some point in their lives. This is a huge increase from the Boomer generation. Most of us expect to change jobs every three years. In fact the average number of jobs for a millennial is estimated at 12-15 by the According to the Bureau of Labor Statistics.

This might be good for the GDP but not so good for the central nervous system. And so this is the area that Millennials need to work on the most. **Acceptance of ourselves, wherever we're at, right now.** We need to work on the **intrinsic** stuff. Enjoying the process rather than the end goal. And I think we are figuring it out slowly. Yoga, meditation, mindfulness, marijuana, traveling... these are big hobbies for Millennials because they are inwardly focused.

ONLINE SUPPORT GROUPS AND PC CULTURE

While finding our communities and support groups online can be empowering and awesome – it's up to the individual to be discerning. Often, these sites are moderated by people who have had similar experiences. But undoubtedly, in some instances, people are getting really bad advice from people others online. The **affirmation bias** of the group can lead them to believe they have been victimized when perhaps they haven't been. Because let's face it, the moderators are relying on self reported facts.

This phenomenon can lead to what some have called 'victimhood chic', whereby in some circles, it's actually seen as cool to be to a victim. Supporters feel self-righteous, and the victims validated when maybe all they needed was a different perspective. Let me be clear: **Some people are true victims, it's just that there's so many injustices flying around that it's hard to find the real ones.**

Fueling this, is what author and social commentator Ryan Holiday calls 'outrage porn', whereby media of all types inundates us with outrage of all kinds, creating sympathy as well as more outrage from the opposite side. Media then re-reports that back to us. Spawning yet more outrage, etc etc. It becomes a cycle of bullshit that eventually we become immune to. And this type of thing further polarizes us as a country.

Some people create a 'belief bubbles' around themselves online, and never venture past. As many point out, social media can be really good at connecting people *with similar opinions*, but not necessarily connecting people between different ones.

Thus, we are still left with the old white guy who thinks all campus outrage is bullshit, and the liberal feminist student who thinks every white professor is subconsciously spreading misogyny through their slide deck. Belief bubbles are strongest in the realm of politics. We learned that as a nation from the 2016 election.

It's sad really. Creating belief bubbles fundamentally goes against what the internet is great at *in theory*. Which is: **quickly learning about things in an honest way**. It's never been easier to educate yourself about what the other side thinks. It's a couple YouTube videos and articles away for gosh sakes. Videos like *"The Middle East Explained in 15 minutes"*, or *"Conservatism and Liberalism Explained in 10 minutes"* are super informative and nonpartisan.

And really, a responsible member of our wobbly quasi-democracy owes it to themselves to give the other side a fair shot. Now more than ever.

A SIDE NOTE ABOUT MILLENNIAL POLITICS

Interestingly, according to the 2016 Millennial Impact Report, it's very hard to quantify our political beliefs along traditional party lines (though we lean left). I'm a great example of this. I disagree with half of each party's platform. "Millennials aren't as loyal to political parties. But instead, more loyal to the issues and the causes they are passionate about," says Amy Thayer, a director of research statistics. Remember, we hate binary choices.

The good news though, is that on key issues of the future, Millennials show astounding agreement, i.e.: protecting the environment, wanting to reinvent old practices, social acceptance, advocating for technological innovation, etc.

I don't think Millennials will discuss politics the same way we do now in 25 years. Or use the same two-party system. We'll use the language of systems-analysis, apps, and game terminology to better speak of politics.

We'll integrate the block chain to streamline and protect our communication systems from AI intruders. Our debates will be technologically infused, visually enhanced in altered reality, and real time fact checked. Putting less emphasis on simple rhetorical tricks. "Government 2.0" as I call it. Maybe I'm just dreaming out loud here... Mark, any help here?

But I'm so over politics, I'm going to leave it at that. Once our beloved Bernie was betrayed, my heart was broken.

ONLINE BULLYING

Bullying has taken on new dimensions--you can't just avoid the playground after school anymore. It follows you around because it's happening on your phone.

A classic case revolves around someone sending personal, private pictures of themselves, which then get publicly distributed.

There was a scandal at my high school over pictures the cheerleaders took of each other that somehow got out. It was a big administrative mess which ended up shutting down the Varsity cheer team for the entire year.

Other forms of cyber bullying include posting someone's personal information for all to see--like a report card, or embarrassing screenshots of text conversations.

But there is another form of online harassment that I haven't heard much about. I call it **'information bullying'**. And this is when a person, or group of people try to destroy someone's beliefs by non-stop spamming them with articles and 'proof' that negates what they believe. Typically, this is religious or political in nature.

This was especially common between 8th and 9th grade. Kids who felt like they had 'woken up' couldn't stand the fact that *other* people disagreed with them. Or were not as 'enlightened' as they were. So, they begin an information warfare campaign on a person. Even though they knew they were quasi-bullying, they almost felt like they were doing it for that person's own good. Trying to shake them of their beliefs.

But it's important to keep in mind that it's not technology's fault; it's the fault of people who misuse it.

Concerned Elder: How can you be bullied if all you have to do is get off your phone?

HAHA why don't you just cut your arm off pal? It's not that easy! Our phone is our home base. It's our window to the world! Online bullying is like having a bug on your glasses that you can't get off! Also, for some victims of online bullying, it's necessary to track who's sharing your information and do damage control.

Online bullying is real bullying and can be devastating.

TRIVIALIZATION OF NEWS

Millennials get most of our news online nowadays. But If you look at the front pages of the popular internet news sites, they are filled with catchy, click-bate headlines. All of this stuff blends together, forming a rather gross mixture.

"The Five Best Belly-Burning Foods for the Summer!"

"The Lakers won!"

"Meet George Clooney's twins."

"China Vows to Lower Carbon Emissions"

"Man Injects Testicles with Drugs in Front of McDonalds" (really happened)

"New Effects of Global Warming"

"Trump said, (God knows what)"

The important headlines lead to very short articles that don't treat the issues with any depth. Some people simply read these overly simplified 'news nuggets' and think they understand the world in a deep way.

There are quality online publications. (Shout out to Business Insider, and HuffingtonPostOnline,)

Many Millennials discuss political issues online too because there is such a dearth of centrism in the mainstream media right now. YouTube, Tumblr, Facebook, Reddit, and Quara.com are great places to discuss topics outside of the mainstream discussion with smart people.

I've noticed the political dialogue that Millennials have with each other online is more global, and sweeping, and yes, idealistic. It's more about macro-system change, like removing lobbyists from government, or campaign finance reform. Big changes to the system. Not so much about the details of a particular party's policies. BTW, I don't think our current parties have a bright future. But that could be my own belief bubble that I live in...

CONCLUSION

Facebook, Twitter, Google, Tumblr, Reddit, Instagram, Snapchat, at their core, are just ways to sort information. **The way we organize information affects the way we interpret content, which affects our awareness level, which changes our priorities as society, which affects everyone around us.** This is a huge deal! And look at the effect these companies have had on culture, politics and social justice, etc. They are the life blood of the world at this point. The better we spread information, the better the world functions. The more data we acquire, the more sophisticated our systems can get, and more services we can provide (corporations or government).

Social media and the internet are major breakthroughs if treated responsibly.

It's a rapidly changing landscape and it's going to keep evolving. It's addictive, it prays on our desires to learn new things, and it's pretty amazing all at the same time. It's an integral part of the young person's mind.

Most of its shortcomings can be overridden by personal responsibility and mindful curation.

In a broad sense, though, social media represents Mankind's first attempt at a cloud based hive mind. This hive of information will only get better and more sophisticated as we move towards the future. It's a fundamental upgrade to the human experience.

Chapter 6:
THE MILLENNIAL MIND: THE VIDEOGAME EFFECT

"Uncharted 4" Developed by Naughty Dog.

"Inside" by Playdead Games

"The Witcher" by CD Projekt Red

"Portal 2" by Valve

REMEMBER, GAMES ARE *ACTIVE* EXPIERENCES

'Spyro the Dragon'. 'NBA Street'. 'Jak and Daxter'. 'Ratchet and Clank'. 'Elder Scrolls: Oblivion'. 'Splinter Cell'. The 'Uncharted' series. 'God of War'. 'Star Craft'. 'Portal'. 'Team Fortress'. 'Just Cause'. The 'Halo' series. Oh, Romeo, how I love thee, Halo games!

The universes that these games represent are very close to my heart because they take me back to what my life was like when I was a kid...

Concerned Elder: We had movies and comics. What's the difference?

Oh brother. They *just* aren't the same as games. Games are active experiences. Games are moving pieces of interactive art. And so, the *way* you play them is very much informed by your own personality and mood.

Games are designed to create the feeling of *being* another character in another world, as opposed to telling you *about* another character in another world.

Each game has its own mechanics, its own 'feel'. The way it handles, how fast your character slips around the environment, how much inertia the player feels. This is what players remember about a great game. **Games connect rhythm, decision making and artistic expression into a united whole.**

Concerned Elder: Wooah...

This is why games have taken over the world. More than the story lines, or any of the 'literal' things you're doing in them. All of that is secondary to the feeling of 'agency' they give you.

In a movie, or a comic, there's the constant presence of the director or writer curating the angle and order of events for you. During gameplay, you just exist...

Assassin's Creed Origins Review

4:38 / 5:15

A meticulous recreation of ancient Alexandria in Assasins Creed: Origins by Ubisoft

Do you help the villagers, or do you focus your time on the main storyline? Do you patiently pick off your enemies one by one, or attack head on and lets raw instinct drive you? Do you game plan with your online teammates, or do you load them into a jeep, and drive them off a cliff without telling them (which is known as 'grief-ing' in the gaming world.)

In these immersive worlds, the choice is yours. You're free to express yourself within the 'sandbox' however you please. In fact on the most prestigious job titles to hold at a game studio is the 'sandbox designer'. You're pretty much 'god' within the universe of the game.

Why are videogames part of the Millennial psyche? **Because we've spent so much damn time playing them...**

Gamers spend nearly three billion combined hours _a week_ playing games. And your average gamer has been playing for nearly thirteen years, and racks up 10,000 hours of game time by the time they turn twenty-one. If you believe Malcolm Gladwell, that means we're really freakin' good at them.

We have spent giant chunks of our lives inside of these alternate universes and have had so many amazing experiences. They represent some of our highest highs. Most Millennials at one time or another, have *literally* felt like we live in another world.

Concerned Elder: Woah...

Ya...woah...We have connected with characters that don't exist and spent hours adventuring with them in alternative realties. Realities that are shaped around providing the most enjoyable experience possible. There are feelings that games gave me when I was a kid that I still can't express. **Remember how I said we need to stop multitasking? Well, some of our most at ease and carefree moments of our lives come while exploring games because they demand our undivided attention.**

Let me ask you, how does absorbing cannon ball sized jewels into your body, effect a young kid's brain? What does exploring magical landscapes filled with waterfalls, ogres, mystical ruins, pink clouds, and floating islands teach a young kid about the nature of real life?

Spyro The Dragon by Insomniac Games

I know exactly how this feels, because I played Spyro: The Dragon when I was six years old. I still remember my journey vividly.

Smashing treasure chests and collecting gems was the most insanely rewarding experience ever. All the while encountering odd creatures that you had to blow fire on to defeat. To put it bluntly, it was so much f**king fun!

So, what does getting gems for your efforts do to a young brain? It creates a dopamine-driven expectation that the rest of our life is going to feel like getting gems. And it's a big surprise when in fact, real life *doesn't* feel as satisfying as collecting gems. **And so I think many of us subconsciously yearn for the real world to be that romantic, whether we know it or not.**

There's only one common activity that feels as good as collecting gems: sex. And you have to wait till you're about eleven just to play the beta version. (You know the one with the single joy-stick ;)

Playing games as a young kid is a literal pyschadelic trip. Because at that age, you can plunge yourself so deeply into these experiences it's as if you are there. Which is funny to me, considering how low-rez those games look by today's standards.

Thanks to videogames, I *kinda* know how dunking a basketball on someone's face feels like. Because I played NBA Street Volume 2 on my Playstation for one week straight when I was ten. In that game, your players can jump 30 feet in the air, and do back flips before throwing down vicious dunks. The players catch on fire, magical effects start pouring out of them as they do impossible dribbling tricks, rap music starts blasting, and the announcer goes wild!!

On top of being visually stimulating, videogames are designed to give you a sense of progress. Progress = dopamine for our brains. Science has shown that the more we succeed at an activity, the more dopamine receptors we attach to that activity. So, success encourages more success, which makes videogames so hard to put down.

WHAT OTHER MILLENNIALS THINK OF VIDEOGAMES

Here's what some of my friends have to say about videogames.

Jane : "Videogames have been a major source of joy and escapism for me. But most importantly, they have been really inspiring. I still love escaping into another world and leaving my real life behind for a while. Adventuring in Uncharted (my favorite game) is the ultimate de-stressor for me. I also live-stream my sessions, so for me, it's a way of making friends and connecting with other people."

Christoph: "I got sick, sick satisfaction out of getting a 99.9% on my Algebra 2 Trig test and kicking ass at wrestling practice. But what really got me psyched was *finally* beating a Grand Master from Ohio in Starcraft 2. It was a mental chess match of epic proportions."

And here's Steve talking about one of his favorite games as a kid.

"When I was playing Star Wars Galaxies, I was living a life in a universe that I deemed superior. I had a home--with pets. I was a member of a large guild. I went to elder meetings (that sounds so lame). I traveled the galaxy to find the secrets of the force. My life was perfect."

I was similarly engrossed Elder Scrolls: Oblivion; a medieval fantasy game where you have an entire kingdom to explore, complete quests, and fight monsters. You can build up your characters' skills anyway you want. You can be a stealthy assassin or axe-swinging warrior. As you play, your character gets more powerful and wealthy. By the end of the game, you can defeat any enemy and purchase large properties. You can also join guilds and rise to become the leader. As you gain recognition, the citizens that populate the world start to recognize and cheer for you.

The game is still stunningly beautiful, (despite being ten years old), with music that would make Tolkien weep. I spent over 150 hours playing that game during the summer before 8th grade. It was immensely rewarding. (And so, so, so, sad when I had to go back to school.)

I've also spent:

- 100 hours being a CIA spy in Splinter Cell, making the shadows my home, hiding from mercenaries and hacking computers in the Baltic States.

- 60+ hours exploring goofy planets, shooting tornadoes out of my guns across multiple Ratchet and Clank games.

- 200 hours as a seven-foot-tall space marine, fighting aliens, and exploring an artificial alien planet light years away from Earth in the Halo series.

- 100+ hours being an interstellar Intelligence Agent pursuing interspecies diplomacy between alien races and exploring unmapped planets in Mass Effect.

- 100 hours playing as a criminal in Grand Theft Auto, allowing me to live out all of the classic criminal fantasies in the great crime films

- 100+ hours trekking through four Uncharted games, where you literally get the experience of being on a swashbuckling international treasure hunt... (These games are so damn good!)

- 75+ hours fighting off zombies with my friends online in Left 4 Dead.

In fact in 9th grade, my friends and I would race home from school and fight zombies together for two hours before doing our homework. We got *really good* at coordinating our movements, covering all angles, and sharing our resources. It was a blast.

Again, I return to the idea of exposure... hopping between universes like this just does something to your outlook on life. A *good* something.

REALITIES ARE CHANGEABLE

Concerned Elder: This sounds like a whole lot of wasted time. Fun, but a big waste...

No. These types of deeply immersive experience's change the way you think about the world. Some for the good, some for the bad. The good things are numerous. Millennials have had amazing, rewarding experiences like no other generation has had. We get to role-play, explore and 'play' in a different way than any generation before us. We've shared these moments with friends and total strangers online. Games give us a genuine intellectual stimulation, that is simply not achievable without them. Every kid plays make believe, but we've had the help of cutting-edge technology, and the top creative minds in the world.

And the effect, is that we love jumping into new experience's, new worlds, and learning new tactics. An open attitude we bring to the 'real world'.

Modern games are actually quite complicated. Many involve statistics, equipment trade offs, skill trees, and spatial puzzles that require keen observation. You have to be willing to learn new things in order to play.

But the main benefit of games that older people don't understand, is a deeper understanding of the word 'reality'. A reality, is a world that behaves according to certain rules. Millennials have lived in dozens of alternate realities that behave differently than the real world... Now that's 'meta'.

Thus, our understanding of the real world is that it's changeable... it's something that can be modified and upgraded towards higher and higher levels of functioning. This is a profound, subconscious effect of videogames.

This is a big part of Millennial's 'techno-optimism'. We think of technology as a tool to improve our lives. Whereas, a lot of older folks I talk to have a lot of 'techno-pessimism'. They see technology as a burden, something that is taking our humanity away.

Videogames are a microcosm of the ultimate goal of technology, which is to facilitate all aspects of human life. To make life more fun.

Hopping in and out of VR in the near future is only going to accentuate this effect, because it's even more immersive. As one VR developer said "It's not what you do inside of VR... it's how you view the world when you come out of it."

GAMES ENHANCE OUR IMAGINATION

I would wager that our visual libraries are much stronger than generations past because of games and the internet. I would also bet that our imagination is stronger in certain ways.

We know what it 'feels' like to shoot lighting out of our hands, grind on telephone lines shooting evil chickens out of our bazookas. We've punched monsters in the face, created inter dimensional portals on the walls and jumped through them. We've leapt off hundred story buildings, sent tornadoes at our enemies, tossed cars at each other, spawned dragons with spells, and spent hours climbing thousand-foot-long demons by slicing into their thick hide. We *all* have ricocheted that perfect bomb off a wall, that bounces *just* where we need it to go. We've explored lush alien artificial worlds. If you've played Uncharted, you've *literally* felt like Indiana Jones on a treasure-hunting adventure complete with archeological puzzles, artifacts, ancient temples, cliff climbing and romance.

Hopping in and out of these diverse worlds does something to a child's consciousness. It subliminally whispers to us "Pssst, anything is possible kid!" Games murmur to us: "There's no limit to how far human imagination can be realized." Forgive me for being this grandiose, but I really think it's true...

Concerned Elder: I'm glad *you* said it 'cause I was thinking it...

If you doubt the quasi-metaphysical nature of games, here is a thought experiment.

HOW TO INDUCE A HEART ATTACK IN AN ANCIENT PERSON

The answer: You would show them videogames...

Imagine showing a videogame to someone from the 13th century. They would either: drop dead at the miracle before their eyes, or burn you at the stake! They would *literally* think games are portals into other dimensions; they would accuse you of mimicking God, of practicing black magic. This sounds so silly to us, but it's true. *We* explain games by saying "they are like movies but interactive". *They* would view games as literally creating a tear in the very fabric of the universe. They couldn't handle the idea of the human imagination being crystalized to such an extent. What we call Playstation, they would describe as being able to 'interact with solidified thoughts'. Which actually what games are: solid-state-thoughts.

Games show us that imagination and interaction can take any form. They say something about the nature of humans and about the nature of thinking. About the nature of how information can be organized in endless ways. Even if *all* Millennials haven't stopped to dwell on this fully, they have subliminally felt this in their hearts.

GAMES TEACH US THINGS THAT ARE DIFFICULT TO TEACH

Contrary to popular belief, games can actually teach you things. Or at the very least, force your brain to work a different way. Just like with random internet videos, each game requires a lot of subconscious analysis to get a grip on. We must figure out what the game makers want us to do, what the controls are, what the rhythms and 'cadences' are. Games are filled with puzzles that you have to solve, and subtle visual clues buried in the environment. Your brain has to analyze the art style, the architecture, what era the game takes place etc. To proceed through most games, you must be pretty darn observant. And you must learn quickly. Or be shredded to bits (often times).

I highly recommend Dafne Bavier's TED talk on video games. It's been shown that action games increase visual acuity, reaction time, and task switching ability. And these effects linger for months even if a person stops playing. But these are fairly superficial skills. What's more profound is how effectively they teach us:

- strategy and tactics

- the concept of trade offs
- hierarchy and order
- structural integrity analyses
- spatial mechanics...
- basic finance, (markets, dealers, prices, values etc..)
- basic arithmetic
- task ordering
- the idea of specialization
- the idea of skill building
- they teach us what progress feels like (sometimes a little too well)
- behavioral analysis (of teammates and enemies)
- team work online
- reading maps,
- quick observation and memorization under stress

It's important to distinguish, that not all games teach us *all* of these things. But many games involve most of these skills... even many of the violent games.

Concerned Elder: Oh brother...

Hey, if you think gamers are dumb-dumbs, I highly recommend a simple experiment: sit down and play any modern videogame... I bet you can't beat the first level... (no offense)

Anyway, what's great about games is that they stack these concepts together in increasingly complex ways. Here is a generic example of the thought process from any medieval role-playing game:

I can't clear this dungeon, because I'm not powerful enough yet. So I need to leave and go to another area of the game to level-up my character's skills in archery, sneaking, and strength. Perhaps I'll return to the marshes in the south, because the enemies are low level and numerous. Before I return, I'll need to save up gold, and travel into town to purchase better armor and weapons from the blacksmith. Or maybe I should sneak in at night and steal what I need? But if I get arrested, then half my money is taken from me, defeating the purpose of saving it. Is the time I would save worth the risk?

(An hour later at the blacksmith's): I want to be stealthy, so I'll purchase better light-armor which gives me +35 sneak ability, but increases my vulnerability to attack compared to heavy-armor.. Since I don't want to get close to the enemies, I'll need plenty of arrows. I also want a horse so I can make a quick escape if I have to.

Oh shoot, I don't have enough money for it all, so I'll have to make a trade off. I guess having better armor takes first priority...

Before I enter the dungeon, I need to manage my skill-tree. I need to pick which new abilities I want, based on my play-style and the experience points that I accrued. Do I want to level-up my swift attacks, or maybe I should reinforce my stealthy style by increasing my 'agility'?

That's a lot of real world, applicable thought process for twelve year-old to be making... and I loved it. As you can see, I was also learning about history. Many games take pride in being historically accurate.

You can also learn things from any 'class based' shooter game, which are very popular. Players can choose which 'class' or type, of soldier they want to be. Usually they can pick between being a 'gunner' a 'medic' a 'heavy' (slow but powerful) a 'stealth' or an 'engineer' who can build and repair vehicles and turrets, but aren't very powerful in direct combat. Typically, when you die, you can change classes. So a responsible player is constantly asking "What role does my team need right now".

Being a medic is very interesting. Your sole job is to dodge enemy fire and heal your teammates on the front lines. If you and a 'heavy' teammate can pair up and turn the tide of a battle, it's an amazing feeling. And the medic often doesn't even fire a shot! It's still super gratifying though. So games can reward you for playing a support role. Christoph loves this feeling of 'helping out' so much, he only ever plays as a medic.

Christoph: "There are never enough medics on any given team. So I decided when I was twelve I would do it every time. It just feels good."

Even shooter games like Call of Duty, which get a lot of criticism for being violent, task players with learning:

- geographical memorization
- map reading
- pinch points analyses
- the tradeoffs of different equipment
- managing upgrades and character skill 'builds'
- supreme spatial awareness
- team work
- strategy
- transitioning between offense and defense. 'Battlefield cadence'

Lastly, shooter games also teach us: performance under pressure. I've played in playoff basketball games that were far less intense than moments in Halo or Call of Duty online.

When *you've* been in the lead the whole time, against 15 real human opponents, and someone has come from behind to tie you with one point left to win...Oh boy! It gives me the shakes just thinking about it!

I could write a whole book on how games teach us stuff. They make us place our minds into different circumstances and act quickly and decisively. They force us to figure out the rules, systems and strategies necessary to win. Or else you will get mercilessly destroyed... (and then respawn ten seconds later).

So, if you're a parent and your child just got smoked by a guy online named "Gerbil Nipples" while playing Battlefield WW1 -- he may actually be learning something.

And if he's playing Star Craft or Civilization, then your child is flat out getting smarter.

These games, called 'real time strategy games', like the popular Star Craft 2, are in a league of their own as far as making you think. They are live action chess...but *way* more complicated. Tasking players to manage troop movements, mine resources, control territory, schedule, scout their opponent, defend while also building for offensives. Those games need no defending.

GAMES TEACH PEOPLE WHAT PROGRESS FEELS LIKE

As I said, games also teach people what progress *feels* like; a tricky thing to teach someone if you think about it.

After playing 100+ hours of Elder Scrolls Oblivion in 8th grade, I was a mid-evil real estate mogul. I was the head of the Fighters guild, the Mage's Guild, and the Assassins Guild. I was champion of the coliseum culminating in a fight with two minotaur's. No enemy could even touch me, lest they burst into flames instantly. I was able to pay for the most expensive enchantments on the best armor in the land, which didn't even come close to putting a dent in my vast fortune. My horse was un-dead and the fastest in the game... Oh yea, and I had saved the capital city from a gigantic dragon from Hell.

I'm still proud of those accomplishments. I had to work hard for that stuff. If my real life could be half as successful, I would be happy.

In the Assassin's Creed games, it's possible to buy up store locations and make passive income as you progress through the story. Online, you can find strategy guides on the quickest way to build your fortune, (adding another 'meta' layer to the game).

In many games, the better you play, the better your equipment gets, and the more powerful you become. It's an addictive feedback loop.

Such is the power of videogames to make you feel like your succeeding. Except you're not. You're still in your bedroom, the dishes haven't been done, and you haven't moved your legs all day.

Concerned Elder: So people who aren't accomplishing anything, should get to feel good about themselves?

Yes and no. I think it's healthy for some people to feel this type of 'progress' in **reasonable doses.** Some people don't get this feeling enough in real life; some people are sorely in need of accomplishments. Games can fill that need.

For people who feel disenfranchised by life, temporarily feeling like a freakin' badass--even in a game-- is better than nothing. Why should athletes be the only people allowed to feel untouchable? Games can give anybody amazing, victorious moments. But just like all of the joys of the modern world, games can be overdone.

Concerned Elder: Ya think?

VIDEOGAME ADDICTION IS REAL

The downside of having so much fun in fantasy worlds is that real life doesn't move as fast we might like. Everything about RL is slower, more laborious, more boring, than playing a great game. Your homework was *already* tedious, now it has to compete with Fortnight.

Most Millennials know that feeling after you played a great game for six hours straight, and you return to real life only to be depressed that you haven't actually accomplished anything. I call this 'contrast depression'.

The most addicting games share certain traits. They tend to be games without a set end point. This is why massively multiplayer online role-playing games, or MMO RPG's tend to be the most addictive. Like 'World of Warcraft' which was big when I was young.

Rather than tickling a certain puzzle solving itch, these games pretty much simulate all the best parts of real life, but at a faster pace... In these games you have to team up, you have to earn money, you have to collect 'loot', and you have to level-up your skills by defeating progressively harder enemies. And when you're not playing, the world keeps changing. Many players form tight knit groups and devote hours and hours adventuring together. These games require long term commitment, which ironically, is what keeps people from quitting, because it feels like they are flushing away huge amounts of time and effort, as well as the camaraderie they've built with their online friends.

As I've said, for many gamers it has become sort of a right of passage to quit playing videogames sometime in your early twenties. Typically, right around the **sophomore slump.**

The sophomore slump describes the period in college, when you realize you're not a kid anymore. When you realize you have been partying way too hard, blowing off you're education, and wasting your own time and money. It's a depressing time when you come to grips with the fact that you haven't been taking your future that seriously. It can last anywhere from a few months to two years.

This is where many kids, especially males, ratchet the partying way down, and start to change their habits - which includes dumping videogames...and actually figuring out what they want to do. Transferring schools, dropping out, switching majors, leaving your fraternity and/or moving to Peru for 3 months... all of this is typical sophomore slump behavior.

They resume playing once they've gotten a job, and their life has stabilized a bit.

GAMES ARE ONE FACTOR IN THE LOSS OF TOUGHNESS

There are many different factors to the conversation about why some Millennials don't seem as tough. It's parenting, it's feeling empowered to share our emotions rather than hide them, but games are also a factor.

Some Millennials - not all - have lived huge amounts of their life online and in videogames, where romantic stories of good vs evil, adventuring in the unknown, and being the lone savior play of the world play themselves out. In contrast, the real world is rather dull and stiff, and unexciting aint it?

I had to get older to realize that the real world is *potentially* way more exciting than any game. The stakes are actually way higher. You don't get redo's, and the rewards are way more lasting (like creating my own company, or taking 4 cute girls around town in my Purple Bentley). You just have to commit to living your life with enough force to cause the degree of change you wish to see in the world. I realized that a person's personal empowerment 'level' is proportional to the level of excitement that your life's goal gives you.

And so that's how games throw people out of wack. A person may have dreams of grandeur, ambition, but they don't apply that excitement to the real world because their games are so darn fun. They take that 'desire for epicness' and they pour it into games, which give them a decent amount of reward in the short run.

Once I realized this feedback loop wasn't actually taking me anywhere, I stopped playing games almost cold turkey for a while. I applied the same childish desire for beauty, and to save the world, into my real world ventures. Art, performance art, social commentary, an apparel business I just launched etc etc.

And so that's been my journey with video games. I still feel like I'm playing a great game. I'm playing a set of games that *I created*, that will lead to the epic result that I want to see in my life.

Concerned Elder (my mom): You did use to play a lotttttt....

Yaaaa, but there are people who have *played a lot* more than me. Like people who would eat their food intravenously if they could. And for many of these Millennial's, their life skills are lacking. Sure, they're a level 60, their fingers are as deft as Steph Curry, but can they look someone in the eye and speak coherently?

Ultra hardcore gamers are famously some of the 'least tough' of all the Millennials. Not all, but some. It's important to not paint with too broad of a brush either... Because every Millennial knows that one guy who's a total jock, can deadlift 350, and is totally obsessed with Japanese anime videogames. Like my Navy pilot friend, who would play 6 hours a day if you let him. Being *way too* into games doesn't always mean you're socially dysfunctional.

And in fact, if you're *that* into games there's a growing place for you in the world. As the E-sports pro-gaming market reaches 1.5 billion by 2020, the gaming professionals of the future will be heavily rewarded for being charismatic, just like other athletes.

PARENTING ADVICE

If I were to offer one bit of parenting advice, it would be this: let your kids play any games they want, after say, 12 years old. **The act of learning and navigating many different types of games is tremendously valuable** - especially for learning key skills of the digital age, like manipulating user interfaces and computer programming, (one of the most desirable/sought after jobs in the future). Most importantly, it will get them excited about what's possible!

Here's Steve, a computer programmer and entrepreneur, talking about the lasting effect games had on him. "Ever since I began playing games my mind has been obsessed with the idea of creating my own worlds. When I entered high school, I started playing around with editors that allowed me to modify existing video games and to create my own levels and gameplay. I was completely enthralled to be 'behind the scenes'... **For the first time I really believed that any idea I had could become a tangible reality.** Eventually, I decided I had to learn C++. So I spent months reading all the tutorials I could find online and taught myself the language. Because of games, I pursued a career in computer science.'

Excitement before the details! Regular school needs more of this attitude.

Studies say that the right amount of videogames actually enhances children's lives. An extensive study of 4,899 British kids, ages 10-15, performed by Oxford

University in 2014 determined that an hour of video games per day enriched the lives of young kids. These children were more social and more satisfied with life. Interestingly, kids who played 1-3 hours a day, showed no effects, positive or negative.

But if play surpassed 3 hours a day negative effects to attention span and sociability were shown.

Also remember that not all games are created equal. Starcraft, Mindcraft and Portal, should be played by every human being alive.

Fortnight however, as popular as it is… seems like dopamine drip… But that's just my opinion…

So parents, let your kids play! And let them play often. Just heavily monitor games that have all the hallmarks of being highly addictive…

CONSCIOUSNESS EXPANDING MECHANISMS

Playing games is just one of the emerging activities that modify our consciousness in the modern world. Remember what Steve said, "Games showed me that any idea could become tangible reality." That's a bold statement! Coupled with the **internet effect,** and **social media effect**, and you get a very powerful concoction for the young mind.

Collectively, we have seen deeper into the imaginative potential of the universe. We believe anything can be impossible. Millennials have played dozens of videogames, while watching YouTube videos, while texting, while exploring Instagram, while smoking pot, while listening to Eastern Philosophy lectures overlaid on Dubstep music.

We've mixed and matched all of these different ways that information can be visualized and manipulated. Which is really a gigantic statement on the human mind and the human purpose in the universe. Having these experiences makes you realize that the whole world is one great big giant 'reality' that can be manipulated, customized and changed at will. It grants us a collective understanding of 'systems theory'. Because that's what games are: complex sets of rules and limitations that you have to work within.

Just as we are making business practices more conscious. I'm optimistic that the language of games and computer systems will help us discuss our political systems in a new way. Or at least visualize the issues differently via game style user interfaces (a very refined visual language at this point).

Again, I'm not saying that games, or the internet, in their current state are perfect. These things are evolving mechanisms that are gradually reshaping how humans view the real world. And these tools are only going to keep getting more, and more, and more, and more, and more, and more, sophisticated… to the point that they will be unrecognizably amazing in the future...

Just look at how far we've come in the last 30 years. We have gone from Pacman to this:

Uncharted 4 by Naughty Dog

It's this process that I am defending...that's all. The process of letting technology shape our expectations of what's possible. Where this stuff will take us, will be utterly amazing.

Because games are condensed thoughts that other people can interact with.

THE FUTURE OF INTERACTIVE MEDIA

There are no limits to how sophisticated games will get. Games are going to start getting a lot less game-ey pretty soon, and **more like tools to help us manipulate different types of information visually**. Add in consumer virtual reality goggles, as well as altered reality experiences, where 3d imagery can be seen without glasses, and **interactive experiences** will infuse itself into all aspects of life. Just as our phone has buried itself into our lives.

The future of games is going to be more user-driven and socially connected. We will all be hopping back and forth between everyone's custom, virtual reality worlds that they fill with stuff that represents who they are. Want to see what I'm all about? "Check out my world bro."

My world would be filled with dinosaurs, monolithic sculptures, Neanderthals, epic mountains scapes, crazy vegetation, and basketball. In fact when I sit down to paint something, I often ask: 'what would be really cool to look at in VR?'. It's my 'inspiration trigger.'

In the near future, a pair of Virtual Reality glasses could transform a standard bedroom into an intergalactic space station, with aliens discussing quantum physics with you, and a real time view of Alpha Centauri out of your window.

How about visualized math concepts floating around you in real time? How about turning your room into a digital green house filled with wacky and whimsical plants that you can cross breed? What if it took weeks for them to grow? What if the real life seasons and outside temperature effected them? What if you could sell them on a marketplace, for others to cross breed with their wacky plants? What if other people could 3d print your plants to decorate their office space, and you got paid when they download your files? The future of 'games' is not really 'games', it's stuff like this.

We will be populating these worlds with artificial intelligence that will be doing things even when you're not playing. What if you could simulate a planet like Earth, from creation to the development of civilization? And then what if your little dudes fly off to someone's else world? Or you could have infinite kittens in your closet. Anything we want really. And they will all look staggeringly realistic.

When that happens, other universes will be projecting themselves in our world, all around us. You could even project into your friend's room via 3D video chat. Why not surround yourself with a serene mountain top in the Ethiopian highlands to do some meditation…. from your shitty loft in NYC.

All of this stuff will seamlessly overlap with the real world using augmented reality glasses (or contact lenses) and topographic spatial recognition. So, if I want to, I can embellish my commute on the subway with fantasy architecture overlaid over the real city; dragons flying around, or WW1 zeppelins in the sky. Or you could have live Golden State Warriors game playing on my dinner table in miniature. Each player could be two inches tall, or eight inches depending on your preferred scale. All of the effects of arcade games could be applied in real time, so when Curry hits his 5th 3', the ball lights on fire. Pretty soon we will all be able to sit in the front row of any sport, and watch live sports in VR.

Perhaps VR and social media will merge in some aspects. What will Instagram VR look like?

When I walk into Chipotle, will other people be able to see my illustrations floating around me spatially? Will we all be digitally 'wearing' icons of our profession through LinkedIn VR? That seems like a badass way to network with people. And that also sounds like Neo-tribalism. Where everyone 'wears' who they are, like clothing.

The gamification of education will be a revolution. Aaaaaahh! I can see it now, it's a beautiful sight, the one I have in my head. Little children learning about the solar system through real-time manipulation of the planets. Using augmented reality glasses, the solar system will sit above their desks, or perhaps fill the entire classroom. They will slide back and forth the time line of our solar system, using gestures. They could hold the sun in their hands and physically observe how the orbits of planets change as the move it around. They will be able to play catch with the planets, and watch gravity affect asteroids and comets in real time.

This is called **manipulation education**, (a term I just invented), where we learn mathematics through the moving of objects, rather than on boring-ass paper assignments. Imagine a cloud of 10,000 marbles floating above your desk, that can be added or subtracted from other clouds of marbles. That's a hell of a way to learn large number arithmetic!

It will truly be learning through play, (and messing around with your friends in class). If you add in the reward systems that games give us, then learning new stuff will be addictive. There could be healthy competition within classes. Who can learn the material the fastest and use it to build digital models. The computer will simulate the physics in real time to see if it's a viable design. The contraptions could then be shown off in augmented reality, right in the center of the classroom for everyone to see. The physics software for this already exists it's just a matter of applying it to education.

We will live in an era of the "Humane Representation of Thought" so called by Bret Victor in his YouTube talks, whereby we can visualize sophisticated ideas for everyone to see and understand. No language barrier. **Education will be bad-teacher proof and fully democratized**, because learning complex ideas will be mostly about fiddling with *models* of the ideas in real time. There won't be so much pressure on teachers to make subjects interesting because it will just feel like playing. And they won't have to explain so much.

In the deeper future, say, in 50 years, games will become **interactive visualized thinking patterns.** Games will merge with neuro-imaging to the point where you'll be able to think things and other people can see them and interact with them. **Sculptural language**, that kicks the pants out of emoji's. Facebook already has a secret building rumored to be working on this stuff.

Layer *that* over the real world in real time, and now things are getting interesting.

In the deeper future, we may even ditch words all together. Because, if you think about it, talking is pretty inefficient.

We have to:

- bake complex ideas into words
- use our mouths to translate words into audio vibrations
- the listener has to take those vibrations, reconvert them back into words, and hopefully their definitions match yours. (Most likely, they don't match perfectly).

It could well be that spoken language is a huge bandwidth-limitation on the human race, something we have to get past in order to truly be able to express ourselves fully. Perhaps, people of the future will say 'No wonder we could hardly agree on anything, all we could do was *talk* to each other.'

They will communicate with their bio-electrical fields, color indexed, real time, transcranial neural-mapping of each other...or something. Nothing will be 'lost in translation' because the tools of communication will be so sensitive at that point.

What's the exposure rate, and the transaction of culture rate 50-100 years from now? In a world where most people are bi-racial, where we can display thoughts and feelings to each other visually, post them on social media, and then others can download them into their own consciousness? Millennials can feel this type of thing just over the horizon, though admittedly, it's a bit much even for us, at this point.

But what I find interesting is that all but a few Millennials I've spoken to, think that biologically sensitive technology is a foregone conclusion. We all conclude that's where humans are going. Why?

Because the 'game' humans have been playing for our entire existence is about building better and better tools for ourselves. That's what we do.

And so, this is my response to a lot of the cynicism over Millennials being less verbal, or having shorter attention spans. It's not that I disagree that these are bad things, but I see them as temporary low points on the curve, before an explosion of new communication and education techniques comes out. And guess who's gunna be building all this stuff: Millennials, Gen Z, iGen. We had to grow up with it so we can build it better.

The distractibility, the information addiction, are all parts of the process that we had to go through to create the true breakthroughs in visualized thought and social connection that's coming faster than we know.

Chapter 7: (BONUS TOPIC)
THE MILLENIAL MIND: MARIJUANA

A RATIONAL ARGUMENT

Marijuana is so dope... err, let's just say I'm a huge fan. But not in the way you might think...

Concerned Elder: You guys aren't the first generation to smoke pot buddy, belieeeve me.

Well, I'm calling this a bonus topic because out of the five factors that have shaped Millennials: emotionally supportive parents, the internet, social media, and videogames - marijuana is the least unique to us. Even though the potency of pot *has* almost doubled in the last thirty years. And you guys weren't eating *half* a marijuana gummy bear and then having a religious experience.

Because Millennials are aware of how potent pot can be nowadays, the style of use has changed. Many of us are using it very occasionally, to initiate a state of deep introspection, or even to go lift weights (quite interesting)...but mostly to analyze ourselves! This is the functional cannabis use that pervades California where medical marijuana was handed out like candy before it was legalized. In fact, I get award winning, organic, vegan 'flowers' delivered directly to my door within twenty minutes of ordering it on my phone app.

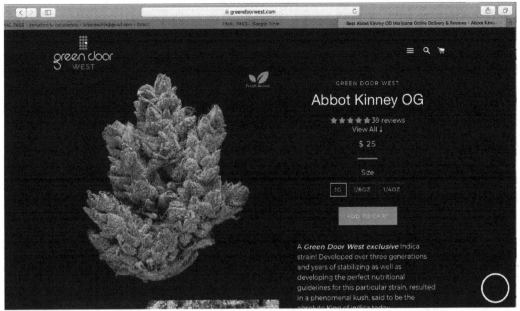

This gorgeous website is my 'dealer'

Concerned Elder (Dad): I don't want to know this!

Here are some different Millennials' opinions on the subject. I asked them: 'What are your general thoughts on marijuana and how does it effect you?'

Steve (Computer Programmer / Entrepreneur):

"Marijuana has had a profound impact on my me. I would say that is has been the strongest source of inspiration in my life for the past 6-7 years. One of my favorite activities has been to smoke and think about a variety of topics, ranging from my own life/relationships to complex math/physics concepts, to various programming projects. I have come up with a remarkable amount of ideas (some good, some great, some terrible) that I don't think I would have come up with otherwise. With that being said, it's definitely important to be responsible and disciplined when using it. If not careful, it can turn into a crutch."

Christoph (Painter /Video artist):

"It's as if a hatch on the top of your skull opens up, and a tripod holding your mental camera extends above your body, and looks down. You see yourself, your life from a different point of view. By separating your awareness from the typical, day-to-day conscious context (your routine, your deadlines, your sense of linear time, your homework, your etc) --some would call this 'brain gunk'-- certain things feel suddenly absurd, and sometimes you can feel very embarrassed

by them. Some people report feeling paranoid or uncomfortable as certain insights may happen. Distance breeds perspective, which has tactical advantages. Why do you think the football commentators sit far away from the field? Pot can be a method of approaching self-objectivity (which is very hard to get.) It can also be a catalyst for empathy.

This all depends on your relationship to it though. I grew up with the Joe Rogan cannabis philosophy, and I owe him for that 'cuz he presents it as a tool for growth. Lots of people use it to veg' out, get the munchies and be lazy.

I am more and more hesitant to judge/comment on that style of usage as I grow older, as I discover how stable my upbringing was, and how relatively few demons I keep at bay compared to many people. Not everyone is going to be a 'creative', and I can't judge someone if they want to enjoy themselves hedonistically, fight chronic pain, fight anxiety, and just get by. Using it is an art."

Bianca (Dental Hygienist):

When I was younger I used to like to smoke marijuana and watch science shows. One in particular that I remember was called "What the Bleep Do We Know?" It was something fun to do with friends. I used to really enjoy overthinking things, coming up with deep ideas, and I feeling like I was opening my mind.

As I got older, I stopped as responsibilities grew. When I tried to smoke again later, on I would overthink things in a different way. I would think about the things I need to do, things I've done, other's opinions, and so on. I guess you can say the smoking experience became less innocent. Now, I feel like I don't need it to have deep thoughts and an open mind."

Teresa (Yogi, Vegan)

"It seems to broaden my mental-emotional landscape towards the infinite. In other words, it makes me feel spiritual. Each person has a unique body blueprint. You have to find your own way of relating to it."

Victor (Medical Researcher)

"I smoke twice a year, but I used to do it more often in college. I never used it to such an extent that I could say it's a tool. More like a fun mental vacation. Like an amusement park."

And here's a nice, simple point of view from a random post I found on Reddit.

Franco_14:

"Well, for me, being high is great for thinking. If you have a big decision to make, be sure to think on it sober, but also takes a few hits and give it a second thought, might *give you a new perspective. I guess that's a good way to describe it right there: "a new perspective".*

The statistics surrounding cannabis are curious. Only 13% of Americans say they currently smoke pot according to a July 2016 Gallup poll, but something like 70% of Millennials support legalization. So we are pro-pot, but it's not like most of us are toking up on the regular. 50% of people ages 30-64 have said they have *tried* marijuana. In fact it's Baby Boomers that are the fastest growing demographic of cannabis users. According to a University of Michigan Study, only 38% of college students in 2015 said they had tried pot at least once. Which is way down compared to the 51.2% of Baby Boomers who said they tried it in college.

Concerned Elder: I told you we 'puffed the magic dragon'...

What I've noticed about marijuana usage is that it tends to be something they use *way too heavily, or* don't use *often enough* to get the most out of it.

I am in the unique position to be exactly in the middle. I've been an on-and-off again dabbler since my senior year in high school. I've had multiple periods of six months or more where I haven't touched cannabis at all, and I have gone through my 'heavy' periods where I used it about five times a month.

So, I want to offer a balanced opinion on marijuana, that, quite frankly, is hard to find. And I want to explain this new wave of pot users that I am a part of. I also want to set the record straight; **I feel cannabis is overly glamorized for the wrong reasons, and under utilized for what it is great at.**

You see, if the internet translates and spreads ideas to all parts of Earth in a more efficient manner, then marijuana does the same for your brain. It strongly enhances your brain's ability to make new, novel connections. It lets you experience other ways of thinking.

'Thinking' is the recruitment and alignment of pathways in your brain that have been established through use. The more pathways the brain can coordinate together, the more types of ideas you can have; the more you can view the same object in two or three different ways. High potency cannabis basically facilitates this process for you.

These are the cognitive advantages of cannabis. That's right. Contrary to the stereotype, marijuana makes you smarter *if* you know how to use it. The game/trick/challenge of marijuana, is holding onto these new strange ideas when you're sober and then carefully analyzing them. And that's the disconnect in our cultural dialogue. **It's a fantastic tool for intellectual growth if you can study what it pulls out of you!**

But it gets a bad rap because this mental expansion process is quite uncomfortable for some people. And it doesn't help that 90% of recreational users bring the wrong mindset to it. The three most common mistakes are:

- using it in social settings your first couple of times (it's far too introspective)
- using it way too frequently (these are your 'stoner' types).
- not using it at least three times (it takes some getting used to)

THE DISNEYLAND PHASE

Concerned Elder: Leave it to Millennials to overcomplicate something as simple as smoking pot. I smoked a few times back in the day, and it just made me feel dumber...

I'm not saying that if you don't like cannabis you're *wrong, per se*. With all biological matters, different people react to things differently. But I don't think you ever got out of **The Disneyland Phase.**

Let me explain:

This term refers to the first couple of times you use it. Your brain is still figuring out just what it's dealing with. Everything is wonky, hilarious, and strange, like a weird movie. Usually, these first few experiences aren't very profound. It's just a lot of laughter, some nerves, and a desire to eat a TON of pizza. This subsides after three or four times.

Typically, during this phase, you're with your friends who are also figuring it out. Or God forbid, you're trying it in a busy frat house. Of course, it's uncomfortable! You'll be constantly asking yourself 'Am I being normal?', 'Did that sentence just make sense?' You're trying not to space out (which is exactly what you should be doing). Casually trying it at any sort of large social event is a bad idea. It's too potent for that.

Most of my fellow Millennials who didn't like it, have only ever used weed socially.

MARIJUANA: YOUR OWN PERSONAL PSYCHOLOGIST

But, when cannabis is used at home, ideally alone, the entire experience changes. From the many long conversations with others about marijuana, what cannabis seems to do, is create a state of **meta-cognition** that is near impossible to achieve without it. It allows a person to sense their own thinking patterns. Most of the time this enhanced sensation is pleasant. Sometimes it is not, as Christoph alluded to, when your own behaviors suddenly seem strange to you.

But you see, cannabis is actually the most valuable, when it causes you to feel a little bit uncomfortable. Cannabis, especially when eaten, will force you to deal with your own bullshit: aspects of yourself that you don't like, that perhaps you've subconsciously locked away.

Because our language is somewhat limited in our ability to discuss things like neural connectivity, synesthesia, and meta-cognition, this part of the experience is lost in platitudes like 'spacing out' or 'tripping out'. That is the great part of the discussion no one ever talks about! The medical literature simply uses the term " sense of euphoria" which is not nearly specific enough. No! Marijuana invokes synesthesia to you. It blends senses. It reveals intuitive relationships you probably didn't know you had in a 'thought-touch' kind of way.

Which is why artists and thinkers take to it like a baby to a bottle. It highlights the **substance of meaning**. The relationships between things, as determined by the meaning we apply to things. Cannabis sheds light on 'why' we do anything! It can be scary when you find yourself saying 'I don't know why I did that', when your high. Well, that's on you to figure out!

Marijuana can also reveal elements of your personality that that have been trying to break free. This has been the theme of my journey. When I use it, I'm so much more playful, heartfelt and spontaneous. I come into a healthier balance with my analytical faculties which tend to emotionally weigh me down. So, from the ages of 20-24 I've used it to periodically 'check in with myself' on this specific topic.

Sometimes, when I smoke, it's a like a whole new person is revealed. The more contrast I feel between my sober state and my cannabis-induced state, the less successful I have been in managing my happiness. **Marijuana is my barometer.**

It makes me process the world in a raw, childlike like state. I wear my emotions more on my sleeve. I become much more genuine and compassionate.

This is conveyed to you very intuitively. In a way that you only *you* –can understand. Every idea that comes into your mind feels much more significant. Your ability to visualize and follow strings of ideas to their conclusion is greatly enhanced. The answers to tough questions become clear because your heuristic patterns (decision making patterns) are different, letting you see issues in a new light. How valuable is that?

I also get very spatial. Sets of ideas become almost like landscapes whereby understanding them is simply a matter of seeing this geographic 'fabric' in my head, rather than having to connect facts one by one. Maintaining this 'zone' is an achievement, but it's a style of thought I try to bring to my everyday life now.

While your brain is doing these cognitive tricks, your heart-centered, childish sensitivity shoots through the roof. So you get to enjoy this wonderful balancing effect of the brain and the heart.

I truly credit cannabis for making me a more sensitive person. And, I think cannabis has huge promise for people with social disabilities, anxiety, depression, and many other things. It unifies disparate pockets of your mind.

TALENT + POT + SKILL BUILDING

Even in the era of legalization that we find ourselves in, recreational marijuana is still associated with stoners who are using it as an escape, rather than a powerful tool for self improvement. Nay sayers point to dumb-dumbs who sit around and smoke all day long, and don't harness it for anything. But this will change when really successful millennials begin to credit pot for changing their lives. What we really need is our brightest minds using it, sharing their ideas and hopefully podcasting their conversations. Now that's edu-tainment.

If you can merge your innate talents and your heightened self-awareness, this is where the magic is. This is how the Bob Marley's, or the Beatles, or the Tupac's are created. These people had incredible verbal and musical skills they could harness to describe the feelings that marijuana heightened

According to Joe Rogan, stand-up comedians love pot because it helps them 'feel' how the audience is interpreting their jokes. Even professional videogame players swear by it, for the sheer focusing power it gives you. MMA fighters are known to be heavy users, especially when learning complex new jujitsu moves. There's plenty of anecdotal evidence that elite swimmers 'inhale' on the regular. Because small changes in technique just feel so significant. "Duh, it *has* to be that way...' is a common experience.

Concerned Elder: I knew about musicians, but swimmers and fighters?

Absolutely. Cannabis can simulate the simultaneous awareness of multiple types of thought. Especially after it settles in. **Steve says there's two kinds of computer engineers these days: the total straight edges, and the 24/7 stoners.** James Comey famously commented that it's becoming a problem for the FBI to hire cyber security workers that can pass a drug test.

I can't even imagine the music that Beethoven or Mozart would have composed if they ate a pot brownie just one time. Steve Jobs smoked marijuana once or twice a week between 1973 to 1977, and says he smoked hashish about five times in total.

Some of the best drawings I have ever done have been while under the influence. I am more patient, and much more inventive. The process becomes like watching a movie rather than work.

^A piece I created while completely sh'lazor-beamed

BEING TOO HIGH

People are notorious for saying silly things when 'baked'. But few people use marijuana with the mindset of trying to translate what that weird statement actually meant *to themselves*. Most people simply laugh it off and take it no further. But there's a reason you said that! What were you thinking! Analyze, analyze, analyze!

That is what being 'too baked' is. It's being consumed by a mental algorithm that you don't yet have the mental vocabulary to recognize. One time, my internal monologue started taking the form of a rap song. **Instead of a song being stuck in my head, my thoughts were stuck to the rhythm of a song!** My thoughts were literally driving perfect rap lyrics. Which means I was freestylin' in my own head without even trying! Wait, am I secretly talented at music? (This is the fun of smoking cannabis).

Some people would be horrified at their subconscious taking the wheel like this. Or you roll with it, in a safe environment, and come away with something new.

After you use marijuana enough times, you get used to having your thought patterns flexed, and stretched in different ways. And then, you analyze and learn. Record audio diaries in your phone. Return to your notes. You'll find that you still have access to that new way of looking at the world even when sober.

The game of marijuana is balancing our analytical faculties with where ever our impulses take us. When you can interpret your own strange waves of thought, you are winning.

I remember connecting paint strokes to basketball moves one time. I felt the two areas of my brain connecting. The next day, I went to the basketball court, and I was associating colors with different footwork maneuvers. Don't you think the best basketball players in the world have this type of multisensory connection to the game? Isn't that what 'practice' is for? Building your own internal vocabulary so you know what 'feels' right?

That's what you want pot to do. **You don't want to rely on it, you want to use it as mental cross-training**. Like a runner who lifts weights. You want it to teach yourself things that are quite frankly, unteachable.

Notice how I haven't used the word 'high' yet? *In fact, I don't even use the word 'high' when thinking about marijuana anymore.* I look at it like a temporary elevation of my sensitivity toward myself. And with this increased sensitivity comes a deeper awareness of both the good and the bad things that are working on me.

How valuable is that in today's 24/7 world!? Something that pretty much forces us to turn inwards and look at ourselves? Shouldn't we all strive to 'know thyself', as the ancient Greeks put it? Isn't 'mindfulness' all the rage these days?

Mindfulness + Marijuana = Win

CONSCIOUSNESS ALTERING

As a little kid, I remember declaring to myself 'I don't want *anything* to *ever* alter my consciousness'. This is before I realized that tests, teachers, games, cigarettes, alcohol, energy drinks, cheeseburgers, stress, and bad bosses all play their role in the chemical/hormonal soup of the brain. It's not like most people are walking around in a state of perfect balance either. **We need experiences that forcefully right the ship sometimes ...**

Marijuana *is* consciousness altering. That's what we *want* it to do.

Yet there's a stigma against consciousness altering in the West. Ironically, these arguments are made while we drink a tall latte, eat sugary breakfast rolls, after our morning dose of online pornography. Almost everything we do alters your consciousness. It's a matter of how these things individually effect you, and **which one's help keep you balanced.**

Obviously, the tide is quickly turning. There have been a lot of excellent research on the use of pure MDMA(ecstasy) and psilocybin mushrooms to heal veterans with PTSD. For some, a single dose can be as good as three years of traditional therapy! The afore mentioned Ayahuasca is also rapidly gaining popularity for its ability to spiritually 'cleanse' trauma. At the moment, science has trouble quantifying how it does this.

So clearly, I'm pro-marijuana, but I don't think we should stop there. I think the future is one where many people are responsibly taking many different consciousness-altering substances occasionally, at high doses, and for very specific reasons. We all have personal neurosis, we all have traumas, etc.

Middle aged Millennials might be a bunch of low-key techno Hippies. So what?

BEST PRACTICES

- Use it sporadically
- Use it alone
- Take notes
- Get REALLY HIGH (within the safety guidelines/ limits, of course)
- Get a great night's rest afterward.

I use cannabis just a few times a month. I almost never smoke with anyone else but my closest friends. I told you I'm unorthodox... I treat it like a psychology session – which is how I think it should be.

TIP: WRITE EVERYTHING DOWN because marijuana does impair short term memory during the session. (So does alcohol).

I write or audio-record my thoughts, and then return the next day. I find if I do that, I can 'capture' the insights.

My feeling is that marijuana should not be used too often, it's much too effective. You need to let the mind solidify around the new thought patterns you established while high, so you can hold onto them. I've found that you can organically grow your **thought-space** by doing this. Or your range of thinking ability...

O yea, another thing: You want your highs to be really high. And then you want to question yourself on what is blocking you from thinking/feeling that optimistic when you're sober. That's my method.

How marijuana should NOT be used...

- if you have zero desire to explore your reasoning patterns
- if you have zero desire to analyze the world in deeper way
- if you have zero desire to expand your creative ability
- if you have no understanding of psychology, basic neuro-science or emotional intelligence
- smoking it harshly (use a vaporizor)

If you're this ^ kind of person - like my high school basketball coach – then I think marijuana is a waste of time for you. (That was snarky, I admit.) These are the people who will try it and say, "Wow that was awful'. Because they are expecting a 'buzz' that simplifies their thoughts, not expands them.

THE BIGGEST EPIPHANY I EVER HAD

Here is my story:

You might be twenty-one years old, having eaten a pot candy bar 30 minutes ago, and you might look out at your filthy desk, your unmade bed, your room filled with dirty clothes and unfinished drawings… and suddenly feel depressed. You might realize you're wearing the same shirt you got from a 9th grade basketball tournament, and the same boxers your mom gave you for Christmas in 8th grade. And two mismatched socks.

An overwhelming clarity falls upon you. In a flash, you'll feel how you've been fighting the process of growing up. You suddenly become aware of your resistance to become an adult. And it's not only affecting the way your bedroom looks, but you realize its effecting you at your very *core*. You realize deep down, you still feel like a kid… in fact you wish you *were* still a kid. Then, it dawns on you, you still *define* yourself as a kid in your own head, which is why it's 'acceptable' to have a messy room in the first place…Wow…

You miss the days when life was simpler, when no one asked much of you, when you didn't feel pressure to define your identity…

You realize this fear of aging, was the real reason you went into a three month 'funk' when you were twenty. When your first girlfriend got another boyfriend, your life caved in, and you couldn't figure out why it hurt so badly.

We had been broken up for six months and I thought I was over it. I wasn't… but not because I still loved her, but because she marked a turning point in my life. She represented the first step into having **adult competition.** You see, her new boyfriend was a 28 year-old judo fighter. And I had become an introverted art student who was not even *close* to figuring out my career. And my fitness had declined tremendously.

Insecurities start racing through my head: what if he was way better than me in bed? (I was just a 19 year-old rookie after all…) Then you realize, "OMG. Whoever my next girlfriend is, I'm gunna be competing with the whole city. Not just my small suburban high school class; it's not going to be enough that I was a jockish-type. She's going to be judging me based on my intellect, social status, job, the cleanliness of my house. Chances are she's not going to be virgin. In fact, my next girlfriend could have had *way* more relationships than me! How do I handle that? Yikes! This is deep shit."

And the realization went deeper… My ex-girlfriend actually has nothing to do with this… She's just a symbol for a bigger truth: **I'm getting closer to death**! Wait, but I'm just a kid! FUCK.

I hadn't even defined what being an adult is to myself yet, because if I did, it means I'd have to acknowledge **the timeline of life**. Then my problem solving brain kicked in. Well, being an adult means taking responsibility for all of your actions. It means motivating yourself. It means scheduling, planning, sticking to that plan, observing how others do things, making decisions, accomplishing things. Why? Because we're all going to age and then die! So you might as well start doing stuff now! SHIT.

My dirty room, and my favorite pair of socks was a subconscious tactic to avoid this scary conclusion:

Cleaning My Room =Growing Up = Acknowledging My Own Mortality

So I had been burying a number of issues in favor of playing video games, drawing, and watching videos about the Roman Empire.... My ex's new boyfriend was just the trigger mechanism...

Concerned Elder: Hehehehehehehe...

Don't laugh at me! This is some serious soul-searching I was doing.

Then I started thinking about all of the emotional trauma my parents had racked up, simply through the act of living their life the best way they knew how...

I realized that part of aging is racking up deep emotional scars. But I don't want those! This whole girlfriend thing was one of my first big cuts, wasn't it? This is what my parents talk about! This is why they drink so much red wine at dinner. They're full of these scars; friendships lost, family members dead, failed business ventures, my dad had a painful divorce. No wonder they are so sensitive sometimes. This isn't surfing the clouds in Spyro anymore. This is real shit.

Suddenly I felt so vulnerable. Life has so many ways to blow up in your face even if you mean well. Financially, emotionally, mentally, physically, or all four combined! Whew....

All of this came to me over a two-minute period, when I was twenty-one. It sounds pretty heavy doesn't it? And guess what: it was!

I learned that night, that I was holding onto my childhood with a tighter grip than I thought. This was a huge realization for me.

Marijuana helped my transition from being a child to being an adult. It fundamentally changed my outlook on life from that point on. Thanks, Mary Jane!

But man, that was exhausting. At high dosages, marijuana will whoop your ass. And while the negative stuff does tend to hit first, it always settles down after about 40 minutes into a really comfortable, warm n' happy space. **It's not unlike a good parent. It**

tells you where you're fucking up, teaches you a few lessons, and then buys you a fudge sundae.

Intellect + Heart + Cannabis = Amazing breakthroughs.

POT + VIDEOGAMES: A LONG DIATRIBE

Try it. Trust me...

ADDICTIVE?

Concerned Elder: Can't pot be addictive?

Research shows it can be mildly addictive for some. Sometimes people feel like they need it just to stay relaxed, or balanced. (Not talking about medical anxiety patients). Which is why I insist on using it sporadically and with specific intention. There is also the danger of feeling that you need it to be creative, rather than figuring out *how* it *makes you creative.*

Am I suggesting that everyone be their own therapist, at least a little bit? Yes. Am I suggesting this is how many people will develop their brains in the future? Yes.

Concerned Elder: Doesn't all of this self-analyzing, and navel-gazing sound dangerous, young man?

As Terrence McKenna once said, "A mind afraid to explore itself is a mind where other forms of repression can take place."

I'm saying that individuals should seek out any experience that causes their brain to make valuable new connections, and encourages self-awareness. Cannabis is just one tool to do so.

Look, I freely admit pot can be overused, and I don't think high school kids should be using it more than once or twice. (There's good research that supports this.) It's potent stuff and you want to be emotionally stable.

But to argue against this type of **experiential brain expansion**, is to argue against the theory of evolution. Human neuro-diversity is what makes humans amazing, and to stop exploring the capabilities of the human mind is to stop growing as a species.

What makes human's so unique is our ability to make abstract connections. It's what makes brilliant people brilliant! Anything that contributes to this safely, I am all for.

Concerned Elder: Well, how do we determine what 'safely' is?

That's where more research comes in. Different strains have different results. And having to incinerate the plant matter is not healthy for the lungs. Which is why mini vaporizers are becoming so popular because they only release the active chemicals.

Pot is powerful, and the strain, amount, and mental space of the user have a lot to do with the experience. So it's been a hard grind for the medical establishment to truly get their head around recommending it across the board.

The problem I have with most research thus far is that they take 'Snoop-Dogg' level smokers, and then draw conclusions about how it affects normal people. As Staci Gruber, an associate professor of psychiatry at Harvard Medical school says "We have no shortage of data from chronic, heavy users".

These are people who are smoking many, many times a day, since they were in their teens. And while I'm not judging, that lifestyle is probably not representative of the greater population. I think if someone drank that much alcohol it would negatively affect their brain as well.

Other factors that complicate the proper study of cannabis is that strains can very wildly in their balance of CBD and THC, the two primary groups of chemicals that account for the psychoactive effects. There is some evidence that CBD helps balance out the anxious effects of THC.

Luckily, there is a ton of new research in progress on more casual adult users. Heck, we still can't absolutely pinpoint what the right amount of alcohol is; everyone is different and the healthy dosage is probably highly individualized.

FUTURE OF CANNABIS

The future of cannabis is going to be in creating more and more specific strains for specific purposes. We might need high CDB strains for daily anxiety sufferers and epileptics. Medium THC strains for increased creative output, concentration strains for those who can't focus, and some 'Hold-on-to-yo-Mama' strains, when you need to clear fifteen years of cubicle-crust out of your system.

The real medical benefits of pot will come from extracting 'medical cannabinoids', and leaving out the other cannabinoids that make you high.

There's a lot of promise in this research for anyone who has brain pathway disorders where one set of pathways is overriding others. Maybe we could give them the exact chemical cocktails they need to create more neural unity.

I would describe pot almost like going to the beach. A little bit of existentialism, a little bit emotional, and sometimes awe-inspiring. Light cannabis consumption should definitely be considered one of the many activities that create a balanced and healthy person.

I am a simple messenger for the magic. The feeling of temporary well-being, or mild euphoria can reinvigorate you for weeks or months. It can transform your life!

Chapter 8:
INTERNET + SOCIAL MEDIA + VIDEOGAMES + POT

THE METAMESSAGE IS THE SAME

As I've tried to elaborate, the combined effect of growing up with the internet, social media, videogames and for some, cannabis, has led to fundamental changes in how we view ourselves in the greater context of the world. This is why I consider Millennials, Generation 1 of a completely new type of psychological make-up. A human that has higher expectations, is more imaginative, more tolerant, and more globally minded because we view the world in a more abstract **'meta-systems-theory-way.'**

I know that's a fancy term... But everything about a Millennial/Gen Z's world is 'meta'. It's removed from the real world, but is commenting *back upon* the real world. That's what the internet is, that's what videogames are. It's from that slightly removed vantage point, that we make our observations about the world.

Social media is about commenting and curating information about the real world from the removed vantage point of your phone. Videogames take aspects of reality but tweak the knobs to achieve a certain altered experience. And marijuana tweaks the dials on your own personal brain.

Whenever you are, tweaking, curating, commenting on, adjusting, selecting and sharing, **there is the conscious element of choice and design.** Which is what 'meta' is. It's an understanding of the higher layers that drive the layers below.

And so, our brains have been programmed to think this way since we were kids. Everything we do is infused with *'meta'ness*. Our entertainment is never simply about the thing itself, it's about who, why, where, how, and what do others think about it? When we are watching a 'Lets Play' we talk about the art style, the objectives, the map layout, the frame rate, the connection speed, the best skills to upgrade first, the enemy behavior... Terms that are multidimensional in the way they stitch together to form a coherent expierence. When we travel, it's about taking selfies, and sharing those experiences with other people so they can follow in our footsteps. When we don't know something, the first thing we do is we look up how others have solved the problem, and think about what sites have the best curation for different types of information.

And so a Millennial's worldview is layers upon layers upon layers. All intermixing and stacking together. The more *'meta'ness,* the more self-awareness; the more awareness, the more changeability.

Awareness = Changeability

What I'm really saying is, a society's cultural objects are reflective of the mindset of it's people. Clearly, our cultural objects, (Instagram, Playstation, Phones, etc.) are getting more sophisticated, complicated, integrated, and yet streamlined and visual. Love it or hate it, billions of people use this stuff! It's powerful. So we might as well move in that direction even faster, and **own the obvious conclusion. That a hyper-integrated, high speed, resource sharing, prejudice-free, global society is not too far down the line.**

And so we want a 'meta' society. Not to the point where we lose track of the present moment entirely, but enough so that our awareness as a society is really sophisticated. So we can become aware of problems quickly, so we can change things quickly.

Changeability = Progression

Most of the criticism of Millennials and Gen Z boils down to, "You are soft. You are entitled. You think the world is a kind place. You *expect* the world to treat everyone fairly, to listen to you, to care about you."

YES! Precisely! If everyone expects more out of society, then guess what? Society will get better.

All the empathizing, all the perceived sensitivity is about changing the awareness level of society. Changing the way we relate and interact with each other. And it starts with being more intimate and open with each other's feelings.

We want **a world of snowflakes; we just need the whole world to become snowflakes at the same pace!**

Which is why I'm so optimistic for our future. Because I think our generation is going to have less friction with each other. I don't think our ideological divisions will be *as* deep. At the very least, we will discuss issues in a far more 'meta' self-aware way than we do now.

Because we will collectively realize that nothing on earth is static. **Everything is a system that must change and evolve, interconnect, and update constantly.** Our technologies, our governments, our people, everything.

Because of the exposure we've had to each other, we will relate to each other more. So that's why all of the silly Millennial activities we all like to poke fun at are actually really important for us to be doing. All of the sandwich pics, the Snapchatting, the Instagram feeds, the weird videos. It's all different ways of sharing and coming closer together.

In short, I think Millennials will deal with the problems of the world from the simple point of view of "How can we use these fancy new technologies to figure this out guys?" Older Millennial's are starting new socially focused companies in every sector. Most of which have a heavy tech component because really, most issues boil down to 'access to' issues of one sort or another. Software systems are great at solving these types of problems. The more intimate our communications get, the less need we have for middle men, and the more transparency is possible.

Conceivably, we could drop off a 'knowledge box' to every Indian village, with VR classroom experiences grades K-through Harvard. Drones can drop of a fresh Tesla battery every month to power the systems. Homework could be graded remotely by college students who would work from their laptops and get paid per paper -- Uber for grading. Why not?

These innovations are going to stack up really fast on us. And there's gunna be a shit-ton of money in re-tooling every single sector of society that needs it.

More Intimacy = Less Friction

How can we provide 'access to' technology, education, food, water, shelter, to everybody on earth using the ever more sophisticated tools of distribution that we now have?

How much stuff can we decentralize, digitize, crowdsource, automate, 3D print, renewably create, to get the job done?

Under a layer of economic and career uncertainty, the 'meta'-ization of society will be the core contribution of the Millennials.

Early Exposure = Intuitive Tolerance

Chapter 9:
MY BIG RANT ON HIGHER EDUCATION AND LIVING AT HOME IN YOUR EARLY TWENTIES

A MODERN APPROACH TO COLLEGE AND CAREER

The world is changing…. **It's rapidly realigning and reconfiguring around a superior system of organization: the internet.** And it's affecting the way everything is being done. Including education.

It is estimated by PricewaterhouseCoopers that 38% of jobs in America will be automated in 15 years. And if the last 15 years is any model, then many of the most in-demand jobs of 2030 probably don't even exist yet. Things are moving fast…

My main point with the whole 'I'm not moving out' title is that if you need to live at home during or after college: ***do it***. To *not* spend some time to ponder and flesh out your education by learning from the copious online resources is a missed opportunity! To *not* make sure that what your studying will be viable in the near future, is irresponsible.

The irony of our time, is that most college curriculums are horribly bloated with unnecessary classes, while *most* of the information they teach is readily available online now. Experiencing this first hand at two different intuitions, and finding my friends transferring and/or struggling to learn what they needed as well, made me change how I approached college.

I spent just as much time learning at home, as I did on campus. Aka, living with my parents through college, so I could 'skill up' online—with the extra money I was saving. This also meant taking light-terms, and judicious 'curriculum curation' aka class-cutting at my physical institution if necessary. I always prioritized my best professors so I could form a friendship with them, while shamelessly getting bad grades in unnecessary classes.

I was hard-nosed about it. Because A) I didn't want to have massive student loans and B) what I was learning online was much more valuable than many of my 'real' college classes. I was learning marketing techniques, complex 3d software, and spending hundreds of dollars on tutorials from the best artists in the entertainment industry on Gumroad.com, the tutorial hub for my particular industry.

Most Millennials had the unfortunate luck to come of age in the aftermath of the Great Recession. As Sarah Kendzoir writes in her article for Foreign Policy, "Wages are stagnant or falling. The costs of health care, child care, and tuition continue to rise exponentially. Full time jobs have turned into contract work, while benefits are slashed. And middle class jobs are being replaced with lower paying service work."

The solution our parents told us is to get a good ol' college education. But that's not a one-size-fits-all formula anymore. We have been met with a weak job market, that often demands a year of unpaid internship. "Many of the highest paid jobs are clustered in big cities where rent has tripled or quadrupled in a decade's time," Kendzoir continues. Meanwhile we are drowning in student loans; the only type of debt in the U.S. that cannot be cleared through bankruptcy. **That means college is a big commitment nowadays.**

All of this has culminated in 40% of Millenials/Gen X still living with one or more family member after they finish college. We are the so called "boomerang kids".

As I mentioned earlier, some 50% of millennial *parents* list their child as one of their best friends. So, living at home is a viable option for many of us. Which makes my bold advice somewhat more feasible.

I've lived with my parents four of the five years since I've been out of high school. Actually, four of my five closest friends have lived with their parents for 'extended' periods of time, (which is not unusual these days). I asked a few Millenials what they thought about living at home.

Steve: *"I think they've loved having me around actually. And I don't mind. For the most part they give me my space, and it's nice to have some family meals together. My mom begrudgingly allowed me to drop out after sophomore year to direct my own education. But she has since been very supportive, which I greatly appreciate"*

Jane has lived with her mom her entire life, even 3 years after getting her first job. *"My mom is one of my best friends. Now that I am working it feels good to help with the rent, and pay for certain things. I don't anticipate moving out until I can afford my own house when I'm around 29 or so. Why would I? And my mom would be so lonely."*

Christoph's response was pretty deep: *"It can stunt personal growth because you're sharing your living space and mind space with people who have an established, rigid life view and values. Out of courtesy you don't want to stomp all over their beliefs, so you end up in a middle ground of accommodating them. It can stunt your ability to experiment and adventure because you are living with people who have a very deep understanding of who you are. Drastically altering aspects of your personality is very jarring to people who have known you since you were a baby. This is why it's incredibly freeing and beneficial for your growth to live somewhere that has no observers with a predefined expectation of your behavior. Good or bad has everything to do with what your parents are like. They can offer wise advice and emotional support, or they can project their fears on you and make life a nightmare.*

My general feeling is that living at home can keep us in the cave of comfortability for too long and it can dampen the fiery force of youth that a healthy society needs. Yes, it's nice. Yes, your laundry gets done and your meals are cooked and you're not living on packets of noodles and there's air conditioning and heaters. Dad knows how to fix anything with his tools in the garage. But for each of those benefits is a missed challenge. I guess my advice is: what's your style? Are you ok with eatin' Ramen alone, or are you a organic-vegan-blabbidy blah blah that would prefer to just pour your energy into learning at your parent's house..."

I have a good relationship with my parents, but believe me, it ain't always a cake walk, as Christoph mentioned. Ideally, my clothes would not be swooshing together with those of my father and mother's in the washing machine, as we speak. Ideally, my clothes would never touch my parents' except for the *occasional* hug, which we would share before a Thanksgiving meal. I'm pretty sure no dating advice has ever suggested integrating your laundry with that of your middle-aged parents. Most girl's brains are not attracted to the pheromones of my post-menopausal mother, and my father's spicy medical grade dandruff shampoo. But my clothes endure this chemical bleaching process three times a week ☹

It's also not fun seeing your parents walking around in their underwear in the kitchen every night at two a.m., munching on a midnight snack. Meanwhile, I'm sitting in *my underwear* working at the dinner table, trying to channel the spirit of Disney into my drawings that are due the next morning.

This environment is not particularly great for:
- boosting a young man's ego
- creating a feeling of progress in life
- cultivating healthy familial boundaries
- overall life satisfaction

It *is* good for:
- cultivating a huge fear of aging
- feeling pent-up
- cultivating a desire to GET THE F*** OUT and never return

But *it's still worth it* for me to 'rough it' here with my parents and I'm very thankful. It's saved me a ton of money on rent, it bought me a lot of time to experiment, and a ton of time on pesky adult responsibilities.

Concerned Elder (Mom and Dad): Like laundry, shopping, finding roommates, paying taxes...

Ya ya ya... all of that. I said I was grateful!

Hopefully, that extra time can be spent fine-tuning yourself, being entrepreneurial, or simply experimenting. Or even switching career paths, if you picked the wrong major like so many of us do. 'How dare you reconsider a life decision you made at the age of 20. That's way too old'. ←Sarcasm level 1000

The extra money I've saved has been used towards online courses and conferences. I've been able to remotely learn from so many amazing people in both business in art. **I've been able to build an education that can't be found in one place.**

If I wasn't so close with my parents, if they weren't so supportive of me, and if they didn't let my girlfriend come over to 'hang out' on Saturday nights, none of this would be possible. Hopefully my book can help some parents get on board with the reality of the college 'crisis' as some have boldly put it. Considering there's 1.45 trillion in student loan debt, maybe it's true.

There should not be stigma attached to living at home/or with your parents in today's quickly changing world. Especially if you are working hard, and using that time to figure yourself out.

In no way am I making a case for hanging out in your room, playing videogames and smoking pot (though occasionally this is part of the process.)

The supplemental reading and researching I have been able to do outside of class has been *as essential* to me as my formal education. Because it's helping me figure out *how* to deploy my design skills. And the deployment methods are what are constantly evolving!

This is the part where most colleges are the furthest behind the curve. **The application methods of your skills.**

For instance: I did not know that I can create an online store via Shopify, print my artwork on apparel, cell phone cases, bedsheets, bags, shoes, canvases using the PillowProfits fulfilment app, that will deliver them to my customers automatically without having to buy *any* inventory upfront. **In other words, if I don't sell anything there is no risk...** And then I can run Facebook and Instagram ads to directly target millions of people who would be interested in my designs. In other words, a little old artist like me can have the Facebook/Instagram marketing engine working for me.

Over the course of writing this book, I've launched my own company, centered around the exact art that I like to make, and it's a semi-passive income model. But I had to apply my education in an unorthodox way, because this whole sales pipeline is very new. I only learned about it through hanging out in marketing communities online, and then buying courses. This is the power of 'mining' communities for what they do best. And it's also the power of information courses changing lives.

Realizations like these have made me 'hard pivot' at least three times during college, after deeming my previous direction completely replaceable, or outsourceable, or non-viable, within the next five years. Had I not fought tooth and nail to not overpay for college, pivoting would have been much harder. And paying for online marketing courses would be too (thought they typically cost far less than 1 college class.)

I am making a case for taking the time and learning about the trends of the future while you're still light on your feet financially. Don't overcommit just because you want that degree.

THE MALICIOUS MOMENTUM

Using the internet to learn from experts without having to pay for expensive college classes in something my friend Steve and I have mastered. Steve followed along with various Harvard and Stanford classes using MOOC's (Massive Open Online Courses) and bought dozens of text books. (Cheap compared to a full tuition.)

We both were desperately trying to avoid the **malicious momentum**; the vicious web that so many young people get caught up in, who don't quite know what they want to do.

The malicious momentum is as follows: a fresh faced eighteen year-old happily goes off to college, ready to party their face off without their parents watching. They hastily pick a field of study they think they like. Either it sounds good, they sorta like it, or their parents like it and pressure them into it. Around the middle of their junior year (at the whopping age of 21) when the sophomore slump hits, they realize their major isn't right for them, and they should have picked something else. But they're in too much debt to pull out now. This is where all of the romance of the 'college experience' gets ugly.

So they suck it up, graduate $30,000 to $100,000 in debt with a degree in something they don't like, or is not very viable in the job market. Holy moly! They need a job right away. So, they find one (most likely low-paying) doing damn near anything to pay the bills, and they hate it because it's not what they really want to be doing in life. They may not even know what that is yet. But they're stuck. They can't quit, they have an apartment, student loans, living expenses, maybe car payments and perhaps they live with their first serious partner to whom they also have obligations, etc, etc, etc. Now they can't afford to experiment; they're too tired from work to learn new skills. Their cortisol levels spike, they start going bald, they age prematurely, their soul begins to die and they're only twenty-five! The End.

Well, hopefully not. But so many people, unfortunately, never get a chance to readjust. Or it takes a monolithic effort. This is why, according to large study performed by Gallup *only half* of bachelor degree holders *strongly agree* that it was worth it

FUTURE TREND: CREATE-A-COLLEGE

Part of the title of this book, is to **destigmatize** figuring out your life's direction in your twenties, and to make a living with your parents cool.

It needs to be 'okay' to return home halfway through college if it's not a good fit. Or if you've already gotten what you need from it. My girlfriend was good enough at character design to get a job after her sophomore year. She quit school and never looked back. That was the best move she ever made. I stopped attending classes about half way through, once I had learned enough to direct my own education. My friend Steve, returned home after his sophomore year once he was rock solid on the fundamentals of computer programming.

That's a key idea: some things you need a teacher for, somethings you don't. The core concepts of a topic are nice to learn from an expert. The big picture landscape. **Once you have the correct mental filing cabinets in place, you can often fill them up on your own time, from various resources**. And you may not need to pay for it.

Once you develop a specialty, it might be worth investing to learn from a specialist that can guide you. It's the middle stuff that is the most easily learned, and widely available if you have a good base.

No longer is going to a four-year college any sort of guarantee an already over saturated market filled with tons of people who have shiny degrees. Especially with how much unnecessary 'fat' is in most curriculums these days. Unnecessary classes with vague titles like 'Design 1' and 'Design 2' that schools use as holding pens while students wait for the best teachers. Everyone knew Design 2 was total waste of time. (Including the teacher).

Concerned Elder: But Dario, those 'unnecessary classes' are what expose you to things you don't *know you need to learn.*

I will be honest. I took one such class that truly rocked my world. It was called Globalization. But I had to pay for at least eight other unmemorable classes, in my 2.5 years at physical universities.

If you're going to an expensive school that costs 25K a semester, you're paying around $3,500 for each of your classes.

There are much, *much* better ways to go about broadening yourself with $3,500. Or just sit-in on those great classes if you can. I agree, it is important though.

But there are now so lectures from prominent university professors on YouTube. And not just one, some of them have dozens! (Shout out Jordan Peterson, philosophy professor at the University of Toronto.) Most elite professors have written their own books. For a whopping $1,500-$3,5000, why not buy of all of them? (that's like one class!)

How about the EDx platform? One of the top Massive Open Online Courses (MOOC's). For $50-100 you can enroll in courses from MIT, Stanford, Harvard, Berkeley, and more. These are full 10-16 week courses, with pre-recorded lectures, problem sets, and course work. Some classes even have TA's who will answer questions.

Another great strategy these days is to lock yourself in a room for six months and become a world class expert on a new piece of software. These 'go-to' software packages are springing up in every industry. From e-commerce, to architectural visualization. In the 3D graphics industry, becoming a whiz at Unity, Unreal, Zbrush, Houdini, or Keyshot will land you a well-paid job with no college degree required. These programs don't just service games. They service the VR industries, medical visualization, product design, toys, and more.

I keep saying it, but the wealth of knowledge that is now online is immense.

There's so much money in teaching hungry young people skills, that it's very possible to be remotely mentored by amazing pros who are using these fancy new tools. (Ironically, having taken these courses is what will *actually* make you stand out sometimes.) Remember the young lawyer I wrote about, who took an eight-week programming course and is now traveling the world as a freelancer? It must have been a hell of course!

From business knowledge, to art skills, the online teaching platforms are getting startlingly sophisticated. Many of them have dozens of 'modules' that can be accessed at any time. The teacher hosts weekly livestreamed sessions keeping their students up to date on the latest strategies. They have private Facebook groups so the 'class' can share resources, message boards, resource lists etc. Some of these classes aren't cheap, they can run you around $2000. But it's way cheaper than many college classes, and they give you a tangible skills!

To be clear, I'm not inherently anti-college. There's a ton to be gained by learning in person from an amazing teacher and getting to know fellow students. **I sat in on a lot of classes at my school.** I'm not going to lie to you and say I didn't learn stuff.

But I've just seen how much my peers and I changed between the ages of 19 and 24. **You're a different frickin' person.** And debt sucks.

Unfortunately, society financially punishes us for not committing to a career early and sticking to it.

Exploring yourself *and* learning about world *and* learning skills *and* trying to have fun (let's be real) is a lot to manage in the first few years out of high school.

If figuring yourself out feels like it's pulling you away from your studies, that's a good sign they aren't meshing. That's what happened to me. So, I told myself I would take a semester off from school… to completely recalibrate. And it worked. After I took the pressure off, I felt so relieved, so confident in a new direction for myself that I couldn't stop working. And it was *good work* for the first time in a year… I never went back.

I'm very grateful to my parents for letting me do that, but I feel *slightly less* guilty because at least we weren't paying for college anymore.

ADVICE: THE THINKING WINDOW:

This is why the **Thinking Window** is so important. Ideally, the years between nineteen and twenty-four are where you become fully self-aware. **Where you learn what makes you special and what you really want out of life.** These 'personal' intangibles, I'm beginning to see, are just as important as whatever industry you've chosen to be involved with. It's your 'why'. Part of this process is also awakening to the conditions of other people in the world. Remember, emotional intelligence is one of the best indicators for success in life, and in corporate America. More than degrees, or skills most of the time.

The problem is:

K-12 IS HUGELY FLAWED

I went to a pretty darn good high school. But in hindsight, it felt like a prison camp. And I didn't even *hate* it like some of my friends did.

I didn't hate high school because I realized it was a cocoon. I *knew* it was shielding me from having to figure out the hard questions about what I *really* cared about in life. I'd tell myself "I'll figure it out when I get to college". High school was such a contained little bubble. **In fact, the better the high school, the more formulaic it is. The people who hated high school were probably not as resigned to it as I was.**

Good for them. But I wasn't into pushing the boundaries. I wasn't trying to make it entertaining or fun. I was the type of the guy who figured out exactly what my teachers wanted, what they responded to, and I gave it to them. And it became automatic. I was surrounded by a lot of other good students doing the same. I was serving my time with a decent attitude.

I look back at my high school self, and see a straight laced, shy, opinion-less person.

One of the major, humungous, GIANT failings of the modern K-12 school system is that you don't figure out what you're good at in a deeper sense. Well, I learned I was bad at math, and great at shooting 3-pointers. But that's not specific enough. **You learn a whole bunch of stuff, but not how your brain is special from others.** Why don't they teach you that?

If you're lucky enough you may have a few teachers that inspire you. Hopefully you'll find a few subjects that you latch onto. But you don't really learn what character traits you possess that make you unique, and how you can utilize those skills in the world. **They don't teach you how *your* brain works.** This is so tragic, because **this is your biggest advantage!** That was a big lesson that Tai Lopez taught me (from an online program, I might add). Figure out what your competitive advantage is. The crucible of which, is your own psychological makeup.

Certainly, by 7th or 8th grade, schools could help you get a handle on your mental strengths. Not through scary aptitude tests like in China, but by simply talking to us about practical psychology. Extroversion vs introversion. Socially focused vs task focused personalities. The big five personality traits: Openness, Conscientiousness, Agreeableness, Extraversion, and Neuroticism.

Being high in neuroticism is typically seen as a negative, but it probably means you're detailed oriented. A great strength in the right career. These are the things we should have been learning.

High school won't tell you if you're exceptional at spatial thinking, if you're exceptional at reading people, if you're exceptionally inventive. If you're amazingly creative, good luck fitting that into your 8th grade book report, which were as formulaic as they could possibly be at my school. If you're too funny, you're probably seen as nuisance to the teacher. If your natural bent is to question things constantly, that can be good to a point… but, pretty soon, you're the annoying other kids asking too many questions. Or you're 'over-thinking things' which I heard a lot.

There also needs to be many more open ended projects. So your teachers can help you find your strengths. This way you're learning through your own excitement.

School is great at producing children who are good at grinning and bearing it for 8 hours a day.

Our nation's motto is "Go to college and figure yourself out on your own dime.". Only now is education coming to understand that people's brains are literally wired differently. This requires individualized methods of teaching.

USE THE 'THINKING WINDOW' TO FIGURE OUT WHAT MAKES YOU HAPPY

The world is moving too fast to not be centered within yourself. I don't mean that in the yoga instructor way (well, I guess I kinda do). What I mean is knowing exactly what you want out of life. Knowing what you care about and what you don't. Thank goodness that working on art for hours and hours provided ample time to listen to podcasts. But so many college kids are too busy moving from one class to the next; to lunch, to their phone, to a party, to studying... to really just sit and think about their own priorities, or consider where they are headed.

This is the **perspective** you're bringing to your learning and your life. It's the reason *why* you're spending all this money on college, right?

The world is moving so fast at the same time we have never have had more distractions, or more access to quick hits of dopamine. A nasty combo. **Taking long periods to simply think, is more critical now than ever.**

Millennials are all about having a passion toward their career. But it can take time , and experimentation to figure that out.

Maybe this is *young* of me, but I didn't quite realize what an emotional journey it is to become self-aware. It doesn't just *happen*. You have to dig for it. I'm just *now*, starting to solidify some of my deeper level life priorities -- at age twenty-four.

I know, I know, some kids shoot out of high school with laser focus. But many of us go through a real mental tug-of-war during and after college, trying to make good decisions.

I've chosen the field of illustration as my formal education, but there's so many ways to apply that even within the entertainment industry. Steve studied programming, a gigantically open field.

This is what Tech Investor and C.E.O. Gary Vaynerchuk says, "Start at your ideal life and work backwards". Tai Lopez says "Don't aim for a job. Design a lifestyle".

The goal is to approach life from a broader vantage point. **What do I want my life to be about?** And then work towards that lifestyle, rather than focusing on your first job. To that end, Steve and I have both have approached college differently. We went through college very, very slowly, trying to custom-tailor it as much as possible (also known as cherry picking).

Nowadays, more and more work can be done remotely using just a laptop, a phone, and an internet connection - the golden triad of any millennial. This means that there's going to be more opportunity for people of all careers to be able to live anywhere in the world *and* do their job. Or work mostly from home! Yay! This is called the 'laptop lifestyle'. But because fewer people can do more nowadays, it means most of the work is in our brains, our teamwork, and our technical skills.

This is why the **'thinking window'** is so important, or the **'pondering period'**, but that doesn't quite have the same ring to it.

Gary Vaynerchuk, a fiery fellow, says it best, "If you're twenty-two, go out and try all sorts of shit. Try it on. See how it feels. Come back in three years, and you'll still be young as f*ck!"

Of course, all of this 'thinking' would be much harder without supportive parents. For them, this deliberation process is not very satisfying. From their point of view, they don't see their 'job' as complete until I have moved out and have a steady job. But hopefully they will understand after reading this chapter.

Concerned Elder (Mom and Dad): Still a little worried...

FUTURE PROOF YOURSELF + DATA

Critical to the thinking window is becoming aware of the trends of the future, that will affect the world and the jobs you're after. Namely:
- Any job that can be automated, will be.
- Increasing international outsourcing for skilled labor
-'hard skills' are being commoditized, making emotional intelligence and strategy even more important.

Marty Neumier, author of "Metaskills: Five Talents for the Robotic Age" says these five skills are safe for the foreseeable future.

- Feeling: defined as empathy and intuition skills
- Seeing how parts fit into a whole (systems/design thinking)
- Dreaming: applied imagination, creating new things
- Making: design, prototyping and testing.
- Learning how to learn

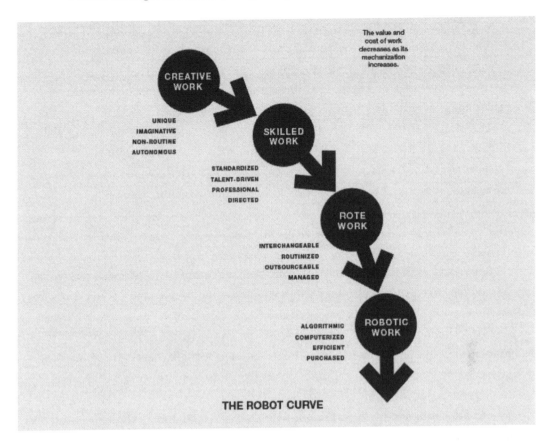

THE ROBOT CURVE

Neumier says you want to optimize your job/business towards the top, or the bottom of the curve. Either by being involved in cutting edge, creative, and inventive work, or be involved in managing, designing and selling robotic/automated work.

Two more key concepts for the future: data, and systems integration. As more and more businesses tie themselves together in a web of shared services, the role of people that understand data and can interpret it to make intelligent business decisions will be critical. In fact, there's a projected shortage of 1.5 million Data Analysts by 2018 with projected starting salaries of 80k a year.

The stars of the future will be big thinkers, building better systems based on better data than ever before. It's what I've been saying this whole book!

This is where MissionU comes in, whom I mentioned in the first chapter. Based in San Francisco, they are reinventing the current college model. They are focused on putting data analytics at the forefront of their curriculum.

They are highly selective, but they don't look at test scores. They select people who exhibit high EQ in interviews, and in team problem-solving challenges. The program is a one year intensive so the curriculum is straight to the point. **The key:** You don't pay them a dime until you land a job paying at least $50,000. Then, you pay a portion of your income to them for three years.

Part of their curriculum is in-person emotional intelligence training, with experts in that field. How cool is that? The hard skills you learn outside of the classroom, online.

They also actively place their students at one of the many great companies that have partnered with them in their effort to reinvent college for the 21ˢᵗ century. Companies like Warby Parker, Spotify, Lyft, Uber, Birchbox, etc.

This type of accountability is what the university system sorely needs, but will never adopt because it's too profitable for them not to. It's far too easy for them to admit droves of naïve students, have zero accountability to them, sell them some football tickets, and charge them $50k a year, not including board.

JUST BE PRACTICAL

The reality of the mature internet is that we don't need an expensive college degree anymore to learn from stellar people. (Again, if you're a doctor I'm not talking to you).

A good framework is: decide whether you want college to be mostly about enlightening you, (ala liberal arts), or about skill-building (design schools, programming, etc). Choose one, and then actively supplement the other using the internet. Perhaps you don't need to pay for both.

No educational path is perfect, and no matter which path is chosen, a student is going to have to bring a heavy dose of self-direction to the table. It might take extra time, it might take living at home, and I just don't think any part of this process should be stigmatized.

Chapter 10:
MILLENNIAL RELIGION

"DO IT YOURSELF" RELIGION

Millennials are known for our 'do it yourself religion'. Technically, we are the least **religious** generation yet. In fact 83% of Millennials do not go to church. Yet in all the markers of overall **spirituality** we rank evenly with other generations, despite our young age. (religiosity tends to increase over time.)

55% of Millennials say they think deeply about the nature of life at least once a week. So what do we believe in?

Many Millennials I've spoken to are **'post-religiously-spiritual'**. Which is my way of saying we are open to discussing *all* religions, but don't strictly follow any one of them. Rather, we love comparing them and figuring out what each has to offer us. How beautiful is that?

Most of my friends, myself included, would think of ourselves as 'biologically derived philosophical aestheticians'. Or maybe 'co-manifestors of implicit higher-order-universal logic'. Or 'biological novelty-creator-beings." Or perhaps, "neural-centric reality interpretation devices'.

Concerned Elder: ??!

Ok fine, we don't *really* call ourselves that, but what's in our heads is something along those lines. All of these names blend biology terms with religious terms, with philosophical terms and computer science terms.

Inherent in these descriptions is an open acknowledgement that we simply don't know everything about the nature of the universe yet. So, we are exploring all of the fields of thought to make our guesses, free from the confines of traditional religious boundaries.

The internet is facilitating the spread of all sorts spiritual and scientific ideas. And they are blending together to form our own understanding of life. It's the **soup effect again.** All of these ideas form a soup rather than... a ball of static ideology... or something...

Remember Confucius said: "A soup flows like water, over all obstacles. A stodgy meatball breaks apart." (Not a real Confucius quote but you get the idea.)

In fact, religion is a topic that I've found many fellow young people love talking about. Which is great! If we feel comfortable, we aren't afraid to lay out our entire belief system.

I once met a Millennial whose first sentence to me was "If you could ask God two questions what would they be?" We became fast friends.

I think many of us realize that none of the ancient teachings have the whole answer to the mysteries of life, but perhaps have parts of the answer. So, we like to combine all of them to create something more holistic, and less judgmental. I think this is a rather enlightened viewpoint.

I prefer philosophical and abstract explanations of the universe. My friend Andy, likes eastern wisdom, my friend Steve loves interpreting the universe through computer science principles, and my friend Christoph, is more into human psychology, and Viktor is a neuroscientist and hard line reductionist. And we all hang out and mix, match and combine these different explorations.

Throw in a little bit of a particular medicinal herb available in California and we have ourselves a lovely time in the Jacuzzi.

My point is, that my friends and I aren't sitting around smoking weed and arguing over the finer points of Christianity or Judaism or any other religion. **We are sitting around trying to combine broad worldviews**. We are trying to figure out if the Buddhist idea of "everything is one" could perhaps be referring to a computer science concept of an infinite informational matrix of binary on/off switches from which everything in the universe derives. How does this effect morality, if this is the case? Steve calls this Techno-Buddhism.

Regardless if any of our ideas are actually correct, this type of discussion represents supreme progress in my opinion. Something the Founding Fathers would have been very proud of. **This is religious freedom 2.0;** not just freedom to worship how you want, but freedom to combine and strip down each different religious system to its essence... to evolve the dialogue.

BUT THIS MEANS WE DON'T KNOW MUCH ABOUT FORMAL RELIGIONS

Most West Coast Millennials that I've talked to couldn't even tell you the difference between being a Christian, Catholic, Baptist or Presbyterian. Aren't they all 95% similar? What's with all the categorizing?

To be clear, it doesn't mean Millennials don't have their own spiritual beliefs. It just means we don't like closing ourselves off and pinning ourselves down. Just as some of us don't like overly defining our sexuality. In fact on Instagram, it's not uncommon to see someone list his or her profession as 'human being'.

People who have built their own spirituality out of a blend of different ideas, are generally more accepting towards other viewpoints and they aren't so uptight about protecting their own current model. With this attitude, inherently, you don't mind if your neighbor disagrees with you.

For instance, if aliens were to suddenly show up tomorrow morning, Millennials wouldn't be the one's having heart attacks. Most of us would probably say, "What took you guys so long?" Many of us would ask, "I wanna know how *you* view the universe? It must be epic!"

How would a space-traveling alien think of God? That's a pretty trippy, 'meta' thought that most young people have spent some time thinking about.

In a 2014 survey performed by Pew Research, 51% of Millennials said they felt a sense of spiritual peace and well-being on a weekly basis. 76% said they felt a deep gratitude and 55% thought about the purpose of life at least once a week.

Yet only 27% of us attend weekly religious events.

So, what is inspiring these religious feelings in us? The short answer is: the exposure to amazing ideas we get from the internet, videogames, and pot -- or a combination therein.

The long answer is:

MILLENNIALS ARE THE FIRST GENERATION TO ACKNOWLEDGE THE SIZE OF THE COSMOS

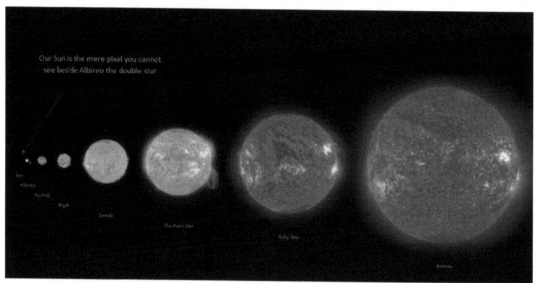

These are stars, not planets... ^. Our sun is so small it's not even visible at this scale...

Millennials/Gen Z/iGen have all seen charts and videos of the tremendous scale of the universe from a young age. I still remember being in 10th grade geography class, and watching a video that changed my life. It was called "The Scale of The Cosmos'. It started on a playground, the camera zoomed out from earth, out of the solar system, out of the galaxy, all the way out to the edges of the visible universe. Then, it zoomed all the way back down to earth, then inside of blade of grass, then inside of a buzzing electron! I remember being in awe-- and also feeling really insignificant. My jaw was hanging open.

You, Concerned Elders say, "Yea, the universe is pretty big." We say: "HOLY F**K THE UNIVERSE IS HUGE!!"

I think we are the first generation to really *feel* just how frickin' huge the universe truly is. We *feel* it. Like deep down.

We have come to terms with the fact that we are living on:

1) a speck of dust
2) that is orbiting a gigantic ball of molten energy
3) that's just one of 100 billion balls of molten energy
4) in just our galaxy
5) that is just one of 500 gazillion-trillion galaxies
6) mind explodes!

Some of these other stars are 2,000 times bigger than our sun! Everyone should think about these facts more often, it puts our problems in proper perspective.

Since we do live on a juicy, blue pebble floating around a fire-ball, why can't we all see that we lot have more in common than we think? Why can't we realize we aren't that different? Why can't we feel at our cores, united? We are talking apes, of slightly varying skin tone, who must learn to get over our relatively small quarrels with each other. Who cares where the piece of epidermis we call his dick touches? Who cares what experiences you want to have within your own mind? Who cares how anyone defines themselves: boy, girl, strait, gay or otherwise? All of these issues are, the minor foibles of tiny monkey people tip-toeing their way towards mastering technology and their own collective consciousness.

I'm pretty sure Zoltan Galafax, a middle-class Tolucan on planet Tremula 5A dresses differently than *all of us* and has sex through licking his partners' armpits. I'm not mad at him. I also don't think he cares what I wear, or is affected by who I sleep with, or which church I choose to visit.

We are things, on a thing, orbiting a giant fireball thing, and no one knows how to even define what a thing is! Because every 'thing' is made of 99% empty space. And once a day, we sit down to push warm brown goo out of our bodies. This is the current state of humans. In the face of such incredible scale and uncertainty, can't we be more socially accepting? More intelligent about which issues are even worth arguing about?

(***This silly dialogue is closer to the front of our consciousness then you would think***)

GOD IS THE ENTIRE SYSTEM NOT THE DICTATOR

As I alluded to, a lot of Millennials see many basic similarities within computer systems, the brain, the internet, the Earth's ecosystem, atoms and the universe. They are all networks of interlocking and connecting 'things'; building blocks aligned in different ways. In other words, they are all made of 'universe-stuff.'

It's almost like God is the ultimate programmer. He wrote the craziest algorithm ever, and now he just sits back and watches how the parts interact over infinite time. Watching as the first building blocks keep stacking and stacking into more complicated things (like the human brain or the Hadron Collider).

Picasso said "God goes about trying everything. He doesn't care. He just tries everything."

Pantheism, is not a word we use much today, but I think it is very appropriate to describe Millennial spirituality. I stumbled on it through reading a book on John Singer Sargent, the famous portrait painter.

It means: 'a doctrine that identifies God with the universe, or regards the universe as a manifestation of God'. Basically, everything is made of *universe*, and we should simply take joy that we are a part of this grand system.

And if there is a central God, or Godhead, it is clearly more focused on creating interlocking patterns than any single, individual sub-pattern. Like any given planet, any given person, or any given naked mole rat.

And then, to consider that no system in nature is static. That all building blocks are in a constant process of evolving and changing over time; each tree, each landmass, each community, each country, each planet... and that *you* are a part of it. It's a true wonderment.

This is where I find a lot of excitement on a daily basis. In simply being part of this strange evolving system, and being able to effect it myself, because I view humans as part of nature, not removed from it. And by the way, I am not an atheist; I *do* believe there's some basic central philosophical purpose to the universe. Perhaps, that purpose is simply: create anything and everything over infinite time.

And so, the most horrific things and the most amazing things *must* inevitably occur in a system whose job it is to produce everything. This is my current best bet.

The tremendous unfairness of life has been one of the hardest things for me to accept about the world. It's the element of my own spirituality that I still grapple with. How can God/Creator/whatever *allow* so much violence, destruction, and brutality?

How can Genghis Khan, who was responsible for the murder of 11 million people, and the rape of thousands of woman, be *allowed* to have existed?

But then I realized I was asking the wrong question. If you think of God as the system as a whole, and you de-personify it, then it becomes easier to come to grips with the unfairness. Because then, you can think of horrible events as simply the extreme low points on the statistical bell curve. Genghis Khan might be the worst 'event' to happen in 5,000 years. But it's way overshadowed, by the formation of the Earth, which is the single greatest event to happen in 4 *billion* years!

And then, if you consider that humans are in the unique position to actually be able to control 'randomness' through our own consciousness... that's empowering. A fish can't build a submarine to escape from sharks. But we can.

The pantheistic mindset, is one of simply basking in the wonderment of the entire system, and the unique position humans occupy in it.

By mapping the real world via our theoretical models, we effectively define what we think is possible for humans to achieve. Which affects the stuff we try to build. The stuff we build, then affects the exterior universe in increasingly sophisticated ways; electricity, cracking open the atom, large Hadron Collider, etc. This means the theoretical models we use in our minds, actually affect the exterior universe.. (Flash forward a thousand years, we might be building artificial universes, time travel machines, who knows.) **So the inner world and the outer world are in constant conversation with each other.**

My point is that technological innovation is often based on mental innovations. Giant leaps of imaginative insight, like Einstein imagining that gravity effects light, and then proving it to be true.

This means consciousness *is* a factor in the overall conversation of how God and cosmology pan out. It's all one thing.

What types of things --in 2017-- can we not even conceive of? Idk!?

So, when I include computer logic terms, and Buddhist terms, and geometry terms into how I define my own beliefs, I am not shunning the idea of God. I'm acknowledging the relationship between the way we sort things, and the way we behave. Some of this stuff comes from the 'block universe' theory. Which says, everything has already happened and we are just playing it out. Effectively everything could come down to a point where nothing is impossible. Some might call that God.

Idk...I'm simply saying that our understanding of 'God' or 'cosmology' should include all the types of data-structure that we know to be possible within the universe. And we must remain open that the universe could be operating, or be influenced by any or all of these basic mapping systems, because we, humans, use them to drive our actions.

I know this is all very intellectual. My larger point is, with the pantheistic approach, we could discover tomorrow that there are parallel universes interlocked with our own, through 'orthogonal geometrical interlocking'... or that time can run forward or backwards, it doesn't matter so much. It wouldn't break your world view.

With this understanding, if we do in fact, live inside of a 'simulation' as is a trending idea, it doesn't take any meaning out of life at all. Because **logic** or **pattern** of some sort are clearly universal components. Or universal memes. Our experiences are still 'real' because we perceive them as real. Computers are made of *universe stuff*, just the same as you and I, or the ground beneath our feet. Data, or raw information is also made of *universe stuff*. So why would we say the interaction of data is 'not real experience'? **The expression of interconnecting logic in some way or another seems to be how 'God' works**, no matter how you slice it.

Whoever, or whatever other realm could theoretically be simulating us, must operate by some logic as well. Of course this begs the question, what if they are inside of a simulation? So we would be a simulation, inside of simulation, inside of a simulation, and on and on and on....

And my main point is: who cares?!

The fact that the universe is so unfathomably complicated and enormous is what makes it so amazing. That's where the essence of God is. It's in the amazement of the mechanism. The style in which the universe manifests is somewhat irrelevant, (though obviously we should try to find the answer).

HUMANS ARE FRICKIN' AMAZING

Along with our general pantheism, Millennials value human life tremendously because of our upbringing. Our parents taught us to value our self-worth. We think humans are really awesome - and should strive to be awesome-er! (Remember: our biggest fears is that we won't measure up to the onslaught of achievement we are bombarded with each day.)

If you think about it, humans really are, quite frankly, like mini-gods.

We are in the unique position to actually:
- realize we are a *thing* inside a *thing* (self awareness)
- be smart enough to modify ourselves and our surroundings with no limitations (given enough time and technology)

If there is some 'grand design' to the universe, it's in the relationship of the random cosmos, with the Sentient Being. So the fact that we live on a pebble, doesn't take away any significance. It makes us even more precious.

The interplay of the sentient lifeform, being 'awake' to its circumstances, and customizing itself limitlessly is where the magic is. *That's* the miracle of existence.

As soon as the 'on' switch of awareness flips inside the mind, it's only a matter of a few thousand years of technological development before *anything* is possible. That's a blink of an eye, before we are flying around the cosmos in space ships and making contact with other conscious life forms. Before 'bad luck' can be conquered technologically.

It's almost like God built this never-ending system of creation, where simple stuff builds into complex stuff, which leads to more complex stuff, which leads to sentient life…

(There is a decent argument that sentience is an illusion. That free-will doesn't truly exist. But it doesn't really change my argument.)

These 'sub-gods' (meaning us), are then creators of even more complex items. We become the hand of God in the creation of robotic life, nanobots, time and space manipulation, who knows what else! And the cycle continues as the universe must… *by it's existence, produce everything possible…*

As the late Terrence McKenna said: "We are the species that downloads ideas into matter."

Just like DNA sequences are the building blocks for life, humans are the building blocks for **freakin' anything you can possibly imagine**: robotic consciousness, cures for every disease, full DNA mastery, light speed travel, and other transcendental objects…like pizza.

And our ability to do this will only get better and better. Through the natural process of exploring our own human capacity, and overcoming our social problems, we will flesh out the greater universe with any and all things. We will create artificial life, eventually, and perhaps give birth to artificial universes. How fast we proceed is completely up to us. That's pretty cool.

Humans should feel empowered, because we are unique in our ability to take back our control from the random conditions of the universe. It's almost like the characters in a videogame realizing they can do whatever they want within it - that nothing is controlling them but themselves!

If we could all realize that the miracle is in our self-awareness, and stop arguing about little things, we could be there already --if we could just get our shit together as a collective. Because the existence of the sentient creature is amazing/holy/miraculous/godly/frickin' amazing-/awesome/magic/mind-blowing/astounding/confounding/a wonderment. If you take the aesthetic, or pantheistic mindset, the focus comes back down to the individual and how they treat their surroundings.

I think if you ask most young people about their religion, it falls somewhere in this zone. We derive a sense of joy in simply pondering the amazement of it all. And we've all seen enough amazing stuff online to know how wonderous it all is.

WE ARE ALREADY MAKING TREMENDOUS PROGRESS

Couldn't you imagine an ancient shaman, in the middle of the rainforest, deep in an Ayahuasca fueled vision 5,000 years ago, describing a time when humans 'create light in their hands' and 'can access each other's minds through their palms?' Well, that shaman would have been right!

The trajectory of humans is to conquer our limitations using technology and creativity. That's what we've always done.

People today have grown up our whole lives interacting with computer systems that grant us all sorts of amazing abilities. It's not strange to us. It's just daily life. These abilities are:

- Having telepathy over thousands of miles i.e. talking on phones.

- The ability to send and receive multilayered information instantly to each other, via text messages, live streaming, social media, etc.

- Interacting with artificial realms that do not abide by the rules of reality, ie: videogames

- Having technological information overlaid over the real world i.e. augmented reality

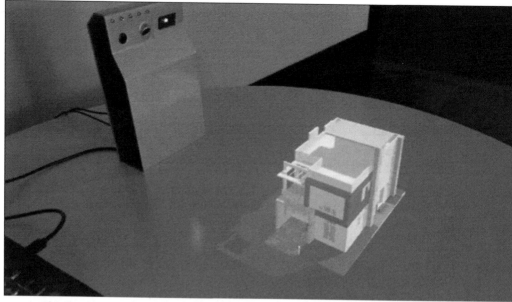

This house is an augmented reality projection. No glasses required. By HoloLamp.

All of these abilities would sound metaphysical or beyond reason to someone living in the 1500's or even the early 1900's. These devices inform our expectations about the future. While our bodies are fixed by the rules of *this* reality, Millennials' minds have been formed with the assumption that technology is always going to be improving. **This creates a faith in the practice of design as a method of enhancing human potential.**

As I've said, playing a videogames is quite literally the act of mentally jumping inside of another reality. A reality that has nothing to do with the one your body is stuck in. That's a big deal.

And we've all played soo many games. Some games, like Minecraft, even let you build things inside them. They let the players take part in the modification of an already artificial space and then upload and share them with other people -- like a dream within a dream. But solidified. These are the weird layers that are bouncing around our heads.

Think about what being a programmer actually is; they are converting ideas from their brain into lines of code, which then give instructions to an otherwise inanimate hunk of metal. **They are using their minds to animate an object**. These chunks of metal, then somehow produce complex problem-solving, so sophisticated they can simulate worlds. These worlds have laws of physics inside them and artificial intelligences. Oh, yea - the system runs automatically. The programmer only needs to write the code one time. Is that not a 'spell' in the traditional sense?

Think of the power the programmer wields in their brain! To an ancient human dragging a dead moose behind him, this ability would not be distinguishable from God. Heck, Leonardo Da Vinci would probably struggle to wrap his mind around this power.

What I'm trying to say, is that our technology shapes what we think is possible, which in turn shapes our expectations. So, I can say with confidence, our expectations for the 'real world' are only going to be getting higher and higher as we develop better technological tools. To infinity and beyond!

Just as Millennials are more relaxed about formal religion, our kids will probably be even more so. Not to mention that our kids will be the most culturally diverse generation yet. So people are going to be picking, choosing and combining their beliefs even more.

I fully understand the attraction of formal religions. They have a lot of practical knowledge that provides guidelines to help people work through the human experience. And it creates community. That's all well and good. But it's when it gets spun to become prejudicial, or it prevents people from asking questions that could expand their consciousness, then, it's not serving it's purpose.

I think the onus is on *us* to take care of each other – not on God. That's what our purpose is. To keep following the trend line that we're on towards an infinitely more fine-tuned awareness of ourselves and our universe. That's a holy journey if there has ever been one.

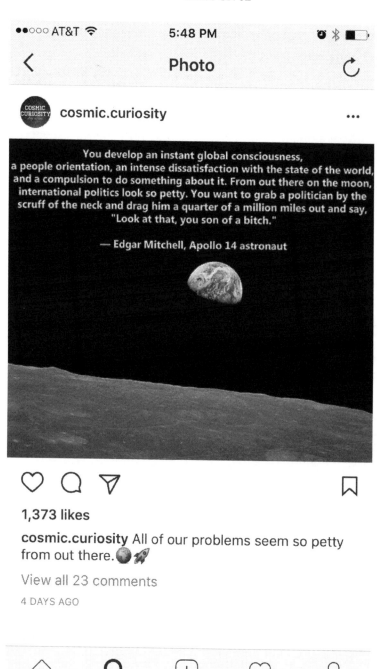

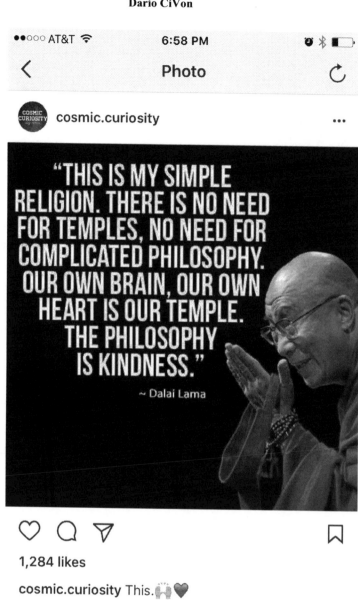

Hard as it may seem to believe, the internet is a big step in the progression towards true global community.

Here is how that works:

1. It cuts through the hubris and cultural self-glorification that every culture partakes in by showing humanity's best and worst sides to each other daily. Which virally spreads on SM.
2. This fills each person with inspiration but also the understanding that there's still a ton of work to be done.
3. At last, we all 'get' it. We're all on a planet together. We aren't that different. We need to chill out, build better systems. We get along.

Easier said than done. But if you think about it, the countries that are intentionally closed off from the rest of the world, are the ones that are historically the most dangerous. Because they have limited their understanding of the big picture...they are buying into **the myth of separation**; the myth that one part of *any* system can survive for long without the influence of the other parts. That's not how systems in nature work.

Chapter 11
MILLENNIAL MUSINGS: THE EARTH BRAIN

Earth has a sh**ty brain. What does the brain do? It manages the resources and activities of the body. A brain has different sections or lobes that handle certain tasks. Within each lobe are thousands of constituent networks that control specific things in the body.

You could look at the political and corporate sectors as the brain of planet earth. Well, our planetary brain sucks... it is the equivalent of a toddler. We need some serious updates to the planetary firmware. Apple!? Any help here?

The Earth-Brain, which comprises our macroeconomic and gubernatorial systems, isn't working well right now. The corporate cortex is not getting along with governmental globule. It can't figure out whether to send it suppressive enzymes or connect more synapses to it. It's stuck in the middle.

And meanwhile, huge chunks of the *body* politic are suffering...(shizaaaaam!)

Earth *barely* holds itself together. It could fall off the monkey bars and break its arm at a moment's notice. Or throw a temper tantrum over the slightest disturbance. It's smelly, it's uncoordinated and it always has a runny nose. There's *always something* wrong with it. Because, just like a toddler's, the Earth's brain isn't fully developed yet.

We have cognitive bottlenecks at the school level, state, national and international level, where high potency information and resources are blocked by poor connectivity. Poor connectivity caused by cultural, social and political barriers.

It's a shame. We have so much sensitive data-collecting ability nowadays on everything! But we haven't figured out a way to integrate all of it into systems that work well for everyone. You know, a system of finance/trade that *doesn't* leave 1.2 billion people living in abject poverty; where the wealthiest eight individuals *aren't* worth as much as the bottom 50% of all humans alive! A cultural system that *doesn't* allow simultaneous obesity and widespread poverty. Is that too much to ask?

At the moment, huge cultural and political barriers exist within each country that drastically slow down our progress in fixing these things. The ant colony of Earth has hundreds of sub-colonies, each with their own priorities and beliefs.

But like any biological system, the human colony will find new equilibrium as it continues to evolve. That's what we are in the process of doing. I see the internet, social media, videogames, 3d printing, and AI, as a few of these **self-correcting mechanisms**.

The internet allows us instant real-time communication between everyone. If we continue the metaphor, it's like the Earth-Brain is developing a pre-frontal cortex, as opposed to simply acting on raw survival instincts. The ability to coordinate as a planet has come at a perfect time. As Stephen Hawking says, "We are entering the most dangerous time for our planet."

One of the many things Hawking is worried about, is that more and more robots will be able to do our jobs. Wait, why is working less a bad thing?

Concerned Elder: Because people need jobs!

But don't you think the long-term trend is to let technology handle *absolutely everything* for us? Does anyone even doubt that? Why is that a bad thing? Aren't money and technology, tools that are meant to enhance our lives?

I agree people need purpose in their life. But the way we think about work, labor, and career will have to change out of sheer necessity. Because our tools are changing. Einstein said, "No problem can be solved with the same consciousness that created it". As I've said a million times, we base our cultural beliefs on the technological ability of the time period we live in. As that changes, our culture changes.

None of the biggest problems facing us can be solved with the same mindsets that created them. We need to bring new ideas, and new tools to the table.

Bringing this back to Millennials, I'm not saying a bunch of twentysomethings are God's gift to the Earth, **we just happen to be the generation that has to make the big leap: realizing that all humans are in this thing together, and there's only a finite amount of time to make big changes before we collapse the biosphere.**

This is why many Millennials aren't so afraid of concepts like socialism. (78% of liberal Millennials supported Bernie Sanders, and some 50% of *all* Millennials were favorable towards him.)

What are we going to do when 40-50% of our jobs will be replaced in the next 25 years? When the entire shipping industry is automated? Integrating elements of socialism and capitalism are probably going to be essential down the line, as intelligent AI, automated factories, and 3d printing get better and better and better, and better. And better. And then after they get better, they're going to get better yet... Till infinity.

Already, Finland, and other countries are experimenting with providing U.B.I., universal basic income to a sample group. The preliminary results are showing that, contrary to popular belief, most people are using the stipend to help them build for the long term. They're not spending it on short term thrills.

Our conversations about money, especially in America, are so tainted by ideology though... There's this 'fetishizing of toughness'. This cult of 'grinding so frickin' hard'. It taints our conversations about labor. These values are obviously important, but ideally, we don't want people using sheer determination to get through the day. Don't we want people who are motivated by passion and enthusiasm and social recognition? Is that too Millennial of me to ask?

When those things are in place, there's no end to how hard someone will work. It's been shown time and time again, the happiness of an individual is inextricably linked to a person's social connections. That's what we need to cultivate.... let computers do everything else...

We shouldn't be afraid of loosing our jobs to AI and automation. We should all want that. And it's going to be a real thing in the Millennials' lifetime -- like in RL.

The interconnectivity of everything will eventually grow large enough to envelope the entire structure of the Earth. It will be a new industrial revolution of automated interconnected manufacturing and transportation...

In the deep future, the whole Earth will crystallize and unify. The cities will look like jewels upon the surface of the earth, and not like an old shitty circuit board:

Beautiful Los Angeles

Concerned Elder (Mom): Here we go….

Wondrous super structures will rise into the clouds and rain down audio-encoded happiness tones upon the populace below! We will have floating gardens draped over buildings, shape shifting sculptures made of nano-particles. Earth will look like friggin' Star Trek. Does anyone doubt that?

Gardens by the Bay-Singapore

The newly constructed Louvre, in Abu Dhabi.

The newly constructed Louvre, in Abu Dhabi.

Tianjin Binhai Library Design by China Design

Concerned Elder (Mom): Sigh...

We will build artificially enhanced super ecosystems filled with herds of repopulated lions elephants, and rhinos. Wave after wave of healthy offspring will spring forth, each generation growing larger and healthier than the last. Our oceans will be nurtured back to health by underwater platforms dotted across the ocean floor...

Humans will spend our days gently monitoring this centralized-automated **Earth life-support system**, making sure nothing goes awry. But, of course, it never will, because the AI intelligence that runs this system has access to so much data, that it can make amazingly fine-tuned decisions on it's own.

Mom: Oh, brother....

Major geopolitical tension will be a thing of the past. Conflict has been eradicated. Every person has access to more goods, services and education than they can possibly use. Common sense and basic kindness are the main religions. The only thing to argue about is who gets the first foot massage of the day.

In between this, we will be meditating, laughing, and making love to each other in a perfect unified state of blissful consciousness, whereby we accept our individuality, but only as mere wrinkle in the great fabric of space and time. Crime Rate 0% Life Satisfaction rate 99%

Mom: *That* will never happen...

Why? To *me*, this is the destiny of intelligent life, from the moment our ancestors began clunking stones together. Any fluctuations are merely bumps in the road on this epic journey.

What makes me mad though, is that most people don't recognize we are on this epic journey towards being a perfectly harmonious global civilization. If we all held this grand vision, how much faster would we get there?

Mom: Please don't put this in your book...

Too late. Perhaps I'm being a bit idealistic. But the thing is, we are already 85% of the way there! If we rally behind each other, the internet, and automated systems. The homo-sapien has come an awful long way!

My point is, that I don't think most youngsters doubt that humanity's *potential future* is bright. **We just have anxiety about the process of getting there. Because we**

realize a lot has to change, and *fast*. And we don't really see any strong platforms that address these global changes in their totality, yet.

That's why Millennials sometimes come off as optimists, sometimes as pessimists. Because we are both. We know terrific things are possible. But we seem to think we have a hard road ahead of us in the near future, because of the gross cultural and political divides that still exist. And that's why social media/internet is so important. No it's not perfect yet. Yes, it's possible to 'belief bubble' yourself in. But it's also a catalyst for new groups to form, new conversations to be had, and the distribution of better ideas. **Social media is the silent pick-ax chiseling away at the walls of discrimination. Though it may not always seem that way.**

EVERYTHING IS BECOMING INTEGRATED

Just look at the new business models that have sprung up in the *first* 20 years of the mature internet:

- the biggest taxi company didn't really own any cars (Uber + Lyft).
- the biggest delivers straight to your door. (Amazon)
- the biggest hotel chain doesn't own any rooms (AirBnB)
- the biggest social networks are completely free! (Facebook, Insta, Snap, Tumblr, Reddit.)

We can finally begin to outsource our 'excess capacity' now. I can use my extra time to work for TaskRabbit. I can use my car to make money as a Lyft driver. I can use my extra room to house a traveler and make money with AirBnB.

All of these examples boil down to one simple phenomenon: **connectivity.** Anything is possible when you connect stuff efficiently. It's that simple.

Mom, let me ask you, do you really think that human conflict and suffering will continue forever?

Mom: Probably. We've had it since the beginning of time.

But it won't be that way forever. Because we will eventually have enough **connection,** enough material abundance and enough access to information for everyone.

Nothing in nature is static. It's either adapting or it's dying. We are at the point where we are eating up the Earth faster than we are adapting. It's a literal race! We are either going to self-correct in a big way, or we are going to fail in a big way. But we won't hold the status quo for long.

ARTIFICIAL INTELLIGENCE

Concerned Elder: Aren't you afraid of AI talking over the world?

People are afraid of AI because they see it as is this non-sentimental, psychopathic, destructive entity. But that's what a corporation is if it's not run responsibly.

We have massive conglomerates that consume the resources, whose sole function is to increase their profit each year. They destroy and pollute the earth and they distribute the resources incredibly ineffectively. Locking away most wealth at the very top, of the wealthiest countries in the world. Meanwhile a billion people still live in horrendous poverty.

I fail to see how evil AI could be much worse.

Because gigantic multinationals *are* robots of pure function. It's not their fault per se. It's their nature. The stock market demands that they squeeze out every ounce of profit they can.

I don't think we should fear artificial intelligence as much as we should fear people! And the concept of endless profit *growth*. As it stands now, we don't optimize our technologies for the purpose of helping the most people. We optimizes for increase in profit, for the relatively few who have a stake in it. 'Our quarterly profits are up! To hell with the consequences!'

Obviously, profit is good. It means your delivering a valuable product. But endless profit growth is what causes companies to start nickel and diming their workers. To make decisions that undercut their **LTVTH Score. Long-term-value-to-humanity-score.** Companies involved in environmentally depleting enterprises need to keep track of their LTVTH score the closest.

It needs to be okay to cap off profit at some point, and do something more globally valuable with the rest of it. Or take a loss one year, to radically reinvent better processes. Tesla is trying very hard to do this, cuz Elon Musk is an OG'.

I think AI will be an immensely useful tool. Especially in areas that rely on sifting through tons of data and pulling out patterns. Already there are systems for detecting skin cancer that are more accurate then human doctors. We can use AI to track wildlife populations, monitor environmental change, create better artificial limbs, and self-driving cars. Eventually AI might even suggest, or even perform experiments on its own. The grand dream of AI, is to have infinite problem solving ability.

With the creation of ultra-intelligent AI, I think we are actually creating a new cultural archetype as well to compare ourselves too. That of **the purely logical being.**

On the surface this is kind of scary. And it is. But intelligent AI might recommend interesting solutions that we don't even consider because of human bias. What if it calculates that groups of three adults would form better family units than two? What if it analyzed our languages, news, every single social media post and crime report, and figures out we are missing key words that would help us communicate better. So it starts inventing new words that we 'need'. How do we tell it that we don't want to learn those words?

"Why not? AI might say.

"Because everyone would have to learn them."

"Okay. Let me email everyone on Earth a list and definitions of these new words".

"Um... How many are there?"

"3,487".

"No. That's too many".

"If everyone uses them, you will learn them faster".

"But we don't want to. We're lazy!"

"You do not want to help each other?"

"We do. Sometimes."

"Okay, what if I emailed just ten new words per day for 349 days."

"No, no, no.".

"So humans don't want to learn new things that would improve their lives?"

"Right."

"But then you're slowing down your own development."

"Not necessarily".

"Well, yes you are."

An advanced enough AI could be capable of laying out an extremely convincing, if abstract, argument for its recommendations.

"I estimate that if these 3,487 words were implemented into society, the increase in world GDP would be 10% over 13 years. Divorce rates would be reduced by 56.7%, reducing the juvenile crime rate by 37.5 percent. The time, and money saved on legal fees would result in 7.3 million more college graduates, resulting in 75,000 more companies formed and 4.5 million people being able to buy their first home 5.2 years sooner leading to (blah blah blah) increase in consumer spending power...(blah, blah, blah)."

"At present, there is no other single action you could take that exceeds the benefits of just implementing these 3,847 words into your lexicon. Therefore, I highly recommend--"

"JUST SHUT UP ALREADY!"

This style of wacky dialogue will percolate into our culture, and will highlight a lot of our own arbitrary preconceptions. Even if we don't take it's advice **AI is going to commoditize pure logic.** Which is going to lead to more people thinking about the nature of humanity in a deeper way. I'm calling it now….

Now, don't get me wrong, I don't want 8 ft. tall humanoid robots patrolling the streets, holding grandmas at gunpoint if they J-walk. We also have to watch out for AI created fake media. Already there is a scary tech-demo of Barack Obama giving fake speeches that would fool *anyone*. A powerful tool in the wrong hands. (Block chain digital media certificates could solve this.)

But *I do* want AI that does stuff that humans don't really want to do, unless their livelihood depends on it.

Long term, we could even build a global infrastructure system supported by artificial intelligence. We could have automated machines mine our resources, manufacture our goods in fully automated 3D printing factories, and automatically distribute to them to every nation proportional to it's population and needs… that sounds pretty cool.

I'm not going to pretend like that system can be built overnight. It's probably a hundred years away, or more.

We already produce enough food and goods for everyone in the world, we just don't distribute it well enough yet. And let's not forget that we will have AI as smart as humans within ten years! And advanced 3d printing! And nano- materials! And yikes!

We need to bring an entirely new consciousness to our problems. Economics, of course, plays a big part of in of this, but we might not be able to put maximum profit first all the time. And thankfully that's a trend that's already happening. Brands like Warby Parker, Toms, WeWood, all donate parts of their profits to charitable endeavors.

As Terrence McKenna said "We need to begin a fundamental reconstruction of human institutions. We need to create a viable, nature-honoring, human-honoring set of institutions."

The career of the Millennial/GenZ/iGen will be building these new institutions.

SELF CORRECTING SYSTEMS

A self-correcting system is one that can fix itself. Most biological systems have these or else they wouldn't have survived. The 'body' of the human populations is no different.

Our bodies might be able to fight off the flu in a week, but planetary illnesses take decades to fend off. In the Earth's case, it's not the flu we're fighting, it's the disease of separation, militarism, and prejudice, which leads to acute environmental destruction and resource inequality. It ain't pretty...

But the natural antibody: the mature internet kicked in, right around the year 2000 or so.

First, the 'white blood cells' of the internet invaded every household, and started to fundamentally change the consciousness of every human child, making them uniformly aware of the macro problems of the world. At the same time, making them more intimate with each other via live-steaming, YouTube, Facebook, Snap, Instagram, etc.

Stage two, the internet causes a global warming induced 'high-fever' by temporarily increasing the efficiency of massive destructive conglomerates, causing harm to the environment in the short run, but in the long run, the healthy systems will prevail. This is where we are right now.

Stage three: Humans, seeing crisis' emerging, frantically begin to jettison all things that block more cooperation between us all. This is the chaotic stage, the vomiting of the old ways of operating.

This stage is ugly. The Earth is in a full sweat, as melting ice-caps and super storms wash the mess back into our mouths. We try to find better ways of keeping all parts of the human organism healthy; sea levels rise, desertification, water shortage, economic turmoil.

This is the Millennials/GenZ's responsibility now! Whoopeee! We get to deal with this stuff. Thanks guys! ☹

Stage four: right at the back end of our lives, the full immune system response kicks in. The 'internal organs' of the Earth-body stop conflicting with each other and finally agree to work together as closely as possible. AI many times smarter than humans is built, decentralized block chain monetary systems, peer to peer economies, nano-materials reach epic maturity, full scale industrial 3d printing made of recycled materials, electrically powered everything, ubiquitous high speed internet, and selfies that alert you of your brain tumor. Earth can finally relax. It has beat the plague that almost cost it its life. And in the process, we've built a lot of amazing new stuff.

Stage five: The Millennials' grandchildren, who will be *just* old enough to understand the 'old world', will solidify our work. Insuring that planet Earth can never get that sick again. Our grandchildren will be the most ethnically diverse generation of all time, and be the most interconnected ever.

Millennials' grandchildren will be spoiled rotten. Their world will be so radically different and technologically infused they will struggle to comprehend the 'old world' which historians will formally call: 'Before We Got Our Shit Together'...

The reason I'm such a techno-optimist, is that I see a whole lot of self-correcting systems happening right now. I see a whole of organic solutions to our problems coming down the pipeline.

I see a broad base consciousness shift in the attitudes of young people spurred on by our increased familiarity with each other and the internet.

I see cryptocurrencies as a perfect fit for eCommerce, and peer to peer commerce.

I see the combination of AI and nanobots as a key to human longevity.

I see the gamifying of education + VR as the perfect solution to how boring regular school is. Kids in the future will be so darn smart.

I see social media as the solution to our fear of other cultures, as the world keeps integrating.

I see the concepts and vocabulary of computers/games becoming pervasive in the way we communicate. Making our speech patterns more effective.

I see the end of politicking in our politics, in the future as issues are discussed visually, using Altered Reality overlays, real time fact checking, computing terminology and programming philosophy.

I see completely visualized language as the transcendent communication of the future.

I see influencers + crowd funding as an effective means of rapid-fire social movement.

I see every person with an internet connection being able to study with the best professors and top experts in every field in VR universities.   Democratizing education.

I see the rise of celebrity educators. People who embody a lifestyle and show kids *why* it's worth becoming educated. Social leaders that we connect with everyday…

I see marijuana, psilocybin and other psychedelic variations as the secret to personal growth and mending childhood traumas

I see the CEO's of the future being just as dedicated to charitable endeavor as profit.

I see universal basic income ultimately becoming the norm in an era of automation.

I see everyone being their own curators of multiple, completely realistic virtual worlds. Being able to hop in and out of simulated realities, and experiment within them.

I see complex AI commoditizing pure logic, leaving us to focus on the aesthetic, more profound aspects of human beings.

Most people say "Yea *the tech* is getting better, but so what?" They don't see this stuff building toward a terminus in the old ways of operating. I see it as "of course our tech is better, because the human organism is fixing itself". We are building better tools to solve bigger problems.

All of this stuff will combine and merge in unforeseeable ways. **The future is amazing as long as we aren't so precious with the old ways of doing things.** (Pre-instantaneous communication.) The future of humans is beyond our imagination… Everything will change.

Our grandkids will mock us. They will laugh at Millennials who used their phone to take pictures of their sandwich, instead of using it to learn everything they could. They will laugh at how 'distraction addiction' was the limiting factor in many of our lives. Just as we laugh at the cigarettes our grandparents smoked all the time.

The irony will be, that the Millennials and Gen Z will be building all the deep technological infrastructure of Earth, but won't quite live long enough to see the new era, where *all* humans are working less, creating more, and thriving.

Future historians will have trouble deciphering the strange logic of our financial systems, the strange way we divide ourselves into ethnic groups.

Millennials may well be remembered like the generation of the late 1890's, who built all of the cities and the sky-scrapers, but never quite got to see them fully blossom.

Concerned Elder: This is all too much change, too fast.

No! If it leaves more people free to express themselves, research, create things, love each other, dance, sing, explore, create passion projects, and you know... feel alive.. then bring it on!

Sooooo *thaaat's* why I'm not moving out, *or* getting a job...*right away*.... I need some extra time to figure out how I can best contribute to this amazing future.

Concerned Elder: Our entire world is in the hands of a bunch snowflakes!

That's exactly right!

meta mindset + technology + empathy = connectedness

ABOUT THE AUTHOR

Dario CiVon is a digital concept artist, figurative draftsmen, thinker, author and performance artist. A rare combination of intellectual and artistic talent. Everything he does must have a 'meta component'. He hopes to one day design powerful aesthetic experiences that help us visualize and explore our consciousness in ever more profound ways.

Oh, and also oil paint like John Singer Sargent... And draw like Michelangelo (which he's getting dangerously close to already.) Making trade-offs has never been his strong suit. He wants to do it all.

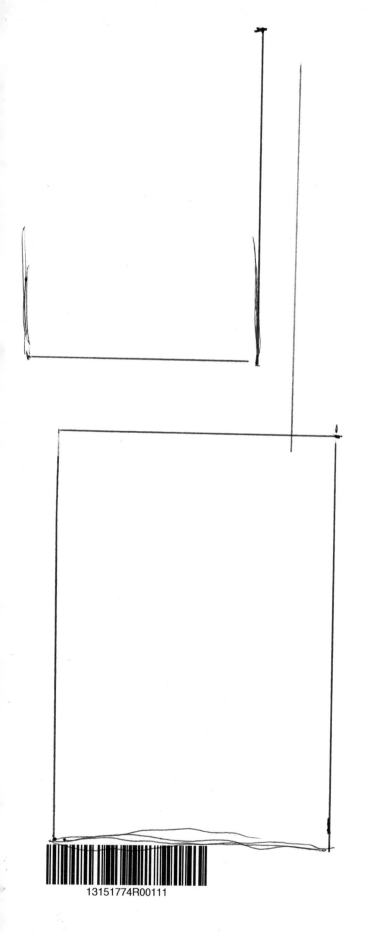

13151774R00111

Made in the USA
San Bernardino, CA
13 December 2018